HOW WE GET FREE

HOW WE GET FREE

BLACK FEMINISM AND THE COMBAHEE RIVER COLLECTIVE

Edited and Introduced
by Keeanga-Yamahtta Taylor

Haymarket Books
Chicago, Illinois

Published in 2017 by
Haymarket Books
P.O. Box 180165
Chicago, IL 60618
773-583-7884
www.haymarketbooks.org
info@haymarketbooks.org

ISBN: 978-1-60846-855-3

Trade distribution:
In the US, Consortium Book Sales and Distribution, www.cbsd.com
In Canada, Publishers Group Canada, www.pgcbooks.ca
In the UK, Turnaround Publisher Services, www.turnaround-uk.com
All other countries, Ingram Publisher Services International,
IPS_Intlsales@ingramcontent.com

Cover design by Abby Weintraub.

This book was published with the generous support of Lannan
Foundation and Wallace Action Fund.

Printed in Canada by union labor.

Library of Congress Cataloging-in-Publication data is available.

10 9 8 7 6 5 4 3 2 1

For
Doris Jeanne Merritt Taylor
1944–1997

CONTENTS

INTRODUCTION

In the days after the disastrous 2016 presidential election, a popular meme showing that 94 percent of Black women voters had cast their ballot for Hillary Clinton was circulated as proof that Black women had done their part to keep Trump out of the White House. The meme, though, was misleading. It was true that 94 percent of Black women who voted cast their ballot for Clinton, but those voters represented 64 percent of all eligible Black women. Even though this was a large voter turnout, it represented a 6 percent drop in Black women's historically high turnout in 2012, when Barack Obama was on the ballot. Indeed, the overall turnout for Black voters declined for the first time in a presidential election in twenty years, falling to 59 percent from its historic high of 66 percent in 2012.*

The search for answers to how the loathsome Donald J. Trump could become president of the United States tended to focus on who did and did not vote. Of course that was part of the explanation, but what was often missing was closer scrutiny of what kept tens of millions of people from participating in the election. To that point, given Trump's repeated appeals to racism, why would

---

*Jens Manuel Krogstad and Mark Hugo Lopez, "Black Voter Turnout Fell in 2016, Even as a Record Number of Americans Cast Ballots," Pew Research Center, *Fact Task* blog, May 12, 2017, www.pewresearch.org/fact-tank/2017/05/12/black -voter-turnout-fell-in-2016-even-as-a-record-number-of-americans-cast-ballots/.

fewer, not more, African Americans, including Black women, have participated in that critical election?

Any cursory investigation into the lives of African Americans would have revealed deep dissatisfaction with their conditions—even after the historic election of Barack Obama in 2008. After all, the last few years of the Obama presidency had seen the rise of the Black Lives Matter movement and an eruption of Black social protest. Indeed, a 2017 "Power of the Sister Vote" poll, conducted by the Black Women's Roundtable and *Essence* magazine, found an 11 percent drop between 2016 and 2017 in the support of Black women for the Democratic Party. The poll also reported that the percentage of Black women who feel that neither party supports them had jumped from 13 percent to 21 percent in the same time period.

To anyone who bothered to investigate the conditions in Black communities, these numbers should not be surprising. Looking at Black communities through the specific experiences of Black *women* would have revealed the depths of economic and social crisis unfolding in Black America. Black women had led the way in electoral support for Barack Obama, and with those votes came the expectation that life would improve. Instead of getting better, wages stagnated, poverty increased, and policing was an added burden.* These very conditions explain why Black women have led the latest iteration in Black social protest.

In other words, Black women's experiences cannot be reduced to either race or gender but have to be understood on their own terms. For example, wage differentials between men and women are often used to demonstrate the persistence of sexism in the workforce. The main statistic cited is that women generally make

---

* Andrea J. Ritchie, *Invisible No More* (Boston: Beacon Press, 2017).

80 percent of what men make.* Of course, that disparity unto itself demonstrates the injustice of sex discrimination in the American workplace, but it fails to capture the enormous injustice experienced by Black women. African American women make, on average, sixty-four cents on every dollar made by white men. In real dollars it meant that Black women were making, on average, $34,000 a year compared to $53,000 for white men.† If we looked even closer, we could see that in Louisiana, Black women were making 43 percent of what white men in that state make. And when you consider that in 80 percent of Black families, Black women are either the sole provider or the main provider, it brings into focus the economic hardship experienced by most Black families in this country. The same could be said of poverty. Black women make up 25 percent of the poor, compared to Black men, who are 18 percent; and to white women, who make up 10 percent of poor people. Thus, the inclusion of Black women on their own terms is not a concession to "political correctness" or "identity politics"; it is necessary to validate the particular experiences of Black women in our society while also measuring exactly the levels of oppression, inequality, and exploitation experienced in African American communities. More important, looking at the condition of Black women reveals the utter inadequacy of what qualifies as social welfare in the United States today.

◆

---

* Anna Brown and Eileen Patten, "The Narrowing, but Persistent, Gender Gap in Pay," Pew Research Center, *Fact Task* blog, April 3, 2017, www.pewresearch.org /fact-tank/2017/04/03/gender-pay-gap-facts/.
† Asha DuMonthier, Chandra Childers, PhD, and Jessica Milli, PhD, "The Status of Black Women in the United States," National Domestic Workers Alliance (Washington, DC: Institute for Women's Policy Research, 2017), 19, www.domesticworkers .org/sites/default/files/SOBW_report2017_compressed.pdf.

The year 2017 marked the fortieth anniversary of the Combahee River Collective Statement, which introduced to the world terms such as "interlocking oppression" and "identity politics." The Combahee River Collective (CRC) was a radical Black feminist organization formed in 1974 and named after Harriet Tubman's 1853 raid on the Combahee River in South Carolina that freed 750 enslaved people.

The CRC formed as a radical alternative to the National Black Feminist Organization (NBFO). The NBFO itself had formed in response to what Black feminists believed was the failure of white feminist organizations to adequately respond to racism in the United States. But the identification of racism alone as a phenomenon in the lives of Black women was politically insufficient as an analysis or as a plan of action.

It is difficult to quantify the enormity of the political contribution made by the women of the Combahee River Collective, including Barbara Smith, her sister Beverly Smith, and Demita Frazier, because so much of their analysis is taken for granted in feminist politics today. Take, for example, the ubiquity of the term "intersectionality" in mainstream political discourse. The Combahee women did not coin the phrase "intersectionality"— Kimberlé Crenshaw did so in 1989—but the CRC did articulate the analysis that animates the meaning of intersectionality, the idea that multiple oppressions reinforce each other to create new categories of suffering.

The CRC described oppressions as "interlocking" or happening "simultaneously," thus creating *new* measures of oppression and inequality. In other words, Black women could not quantify their oppression only in terms of sexism or racism, or of homophobia experienced by Black lesbians. They were not ever a single category, but it was the merging or enmeshment of those identities that compounded how Black women experienced oppression.

The women of the CRC were not the first Black women to recognize their position in American society. This historic insight was captured, perhaps most succinctly, by Black writer and public intellectual Anna Julia Cooper in 1892: "The colored woman of to-day occupies . . . a unique position in this country. . . . She is confronted by both a woman question and a race problem, and is as yet an unknown or an unacknowledged factor in both."* In the 1960s, Black feminist activists like Frances Beal described the oppression of Black women as "double jeopardy," which also recognized the specificity of their compounded oppressions.

The Combahee River Collective built on those observations by continuing to analyze the roots of Black women's oppression under capitalism and arguing for the reorganization of society based on the collective needs of the most oppressed. That is to say, if you could free the most oppressed people in society, then you would have to free everyone. For the Combahee River Collective, this was not an academic exercise. Not only was it crucial to understanding the particular experiences of Black women as compared to white women and Black men, but it also created entry points for Black women to engage in politics. This was a critical aspect of the CRC's political intervention in the women's movement. One could not expect Black women to be wholly active in political movements that neither represented nor advanced their interests. The inability or unwillingness of most white feminist organizations to fully engage with antiracist issues affecting Black women, like campaigning against sterilization and sexual assault or for low-wage labor and workplace rights, alienated Black women and other women of color from becoming active in those organizations.

---

* Anna Julia Cooper, "The Status of Woman in America," in *A Voice From the South* (New York: Oxford University Press, 1990), 134; Brittney C. Cooper, *Beyond Respectability: The Intellectual Thought of Race Women* (Urbana, IL: University of Illinois Press, 2017).

The same was true within the Black liberation movement that was overwhelmingly dominated by Black men. Indeed, it was not unusual for Black male organizers to oppose abortion rights for Black women on the basis that abortion was genocide for Black people. Thus, the narrow agendas of white liberal feminist organizations and some purported Black radical organizations cut them off from a cadre of radical Black women who had been politically trained through their participation in the civil rights movement and the urban-based Black insurgency during most of the 1960s. The inattention to Black women's issues also cut them off from newly radicalizing Black women looking to become involved in political activism. In this context, the women of Combahee were not only making a political intervention into the feminist movement, but by doing so, they were also creating new entry points into activism for Black and Brown women who would have otherwise been ignored. This was borne out in Boston, for example, where the Combahee River Collective was centrally involved in campaigns against the sterilization of Black and Brown women, the abortion rights movement, and the emergent struggle against domestic violence. Of course, all of these women newly activated into the feminist movement did not join the CRC, yet the influence of that organization and the generalization of their analysis opened up the world of organizing and radical politics to new Black feminists.

Demita Frazier, for example, had been active in the Black Panther Party in Chicago long before she was involved in the CRC. Barbara Smith cut her political teeth in the antiwar movement and as a fellow traveler of the socialist left and Students for a Democratic Society (SDS). Beverly Smith had been active in the Congress on Racial Equality in Cleveland. In all of their cases and perhaps thousands of others, these women had come to revolutionary conclusions that their, and indeed all Black people's, oppression was rooted deeply in capitalism. This meant that the narrow goals of simply reaching "equality" with men or with white people were not enough. It also meant that many Black feminists rejected the calls for women to completely separate from men, as lesbian separatists advocated. Black men and women may experience racism differently in the world, but they had common interests in overcoming it—interests that could not be realized in struggles separated along the lines of gender. The point was to convince Black men that their interests were also tied to the liberation of Black women and that they should play an active role in that struggle.

The radicalization of African Americans over the course of the 1960s brought many of them to revolutionary conclusions. They came to believe that Black liberation could not actually be achieved within the confines of capitalist society. While predominantly Black male–led and -dominated organizations have historically been presented as the vessels for these kinds of politics, radical and revolutionary Black feminist organizations took up these politics well into the 1970s.

The Combahee River Collective Statement stands tall among the many statements, manifestos, and other public declarations of the period for its clarity, rigor, and political reach. It is an important document, not only as a statement of radical Black feminism but also in its contribution to the revolutionary left in the United States. The main reason is that the women of Combahee not only saw themselves as "radicals" but also considered themselves socialists. They were not acting or writing against Marxism, but, in their own words, they looked to "extend" Marxist analysis to incorporate an understanding of the oppression of Black women. In doing so, they have sharpened Marxist analysis by recognizing the plight of Black women as an oppressed group that has particular political needs. As they wrote, "We are not convinced . . .

that a socialist revolution that is not also a feminist and antiracist revolution will guarantee our liberation."

The CRC identified their recognition of this political tension as "identity politics." The CRC statement is believed to be the first text where the term "identity politics" is used. Since 1977, that term has been used, abused, and reconfigured into something foreign to its creators. The CRC made two key observations in their use of "identity politics." The first was that oppression on the basis of identity—whether it was racial, gender, class, or sexual orientation identity—was a source of political radicalization. Black women were not radicalizing over abstract issues of doctrine; they were radicalizing because of the ways that their multiple identities opened them up to overlapping oppression and exploitation. Black women's social positions made them disproportionately susceptible to the ravages of capitalism, including poverty, illness, violence, sexual assault, and inadequate healthcare and housing, to name only the most obvious. These vulnerabilities also made Black women more skeptical of the political status quo and, in many cases, of capitalism itself. In other words, Black women's oppression made them more open to the possibilities of radical politics and activism.

The Marxist tradition had also recognized this dynamic when Russian revolutionary Vladimir Lenin identified the "special oppression" of national minorities as an added burden they faced. Lenin used this framework of "special oppression" to call upon the Communist Party in the 1920s to become more active in the struggles of Black people against racism.* Lenin also recognized that the layers of oppression faced by Black people made them, potentially, more curious about and open to the arguments of the Communists.

---

* Jacob Zumoff, *The Communist International and US Communism*, 1919–1929 (Leiden, Netherlands: Brill, 2014), 292–93.

But "identity politics" was not just about who you were; it was also about what you could do to confront the oppression you were facing. Or, as Black women had argued within the broader feminist movement: "the personal is political." This slogan was not just about "lifestyle" issues, as it came to be popularly understood, rather it was initially about how the experiences within the lives of Black women shaped their political outlook. The experiences of oppression, humiliations, and the indignities created by poverty, racism, and sexism opened Black women up to the possibility of radical and revolutionary politics. This is, perhaps, why Black feminists identified reproductive justice as a priority, from abortion rights to ending the sterilization practices that were common in gynecological medicine when it came to treating working-class Black and Puerto Rican women in the United States, including Puerto Rico. Identity politics became a way that those suffering that oppression could become politically active to confront it. This meant taking up political campaigns not just to ensure the liberation of other people but also to guarantee your own freedom. It was also of critical importance that the CRC statement identified "class oppression" as central to the experience of Black women, as in doing so they helped to distinguish radical Black feminist politics from a developing middle-class orientation in Black politics that was on the ascent in the 1970s. Indeed, the intersecting factors of race, gender, and class meant that Black women were over-represented in the ranks of the poor and working class.

Combahee's grasp of the centrality of class in Black women's lives was not only based in history but was also in anticipation of its growing potential as a key divide even among Black women. Today that could not be clearer. The number of Black women who are wealthy and elite is small, but they are extremely visible and influential. From Michelle Obama to Oprah Winfrey to US senator Kamala Harris, they, as so many other Black wealthy and influential people, are held up as examples of American capitalism as just and democratic. They are represented as the hope that the United States can still deliver the American Dream. For example, in the summer of 2016 Michelle Obama delivered a speech at the Democratic National Convention that electrified her audience, as she outlined what she believed to be evidence of American progress. She described how "the generations of people who felt the lash of bondage, the shame of servitude, the sting of segregation . . . kept striving . . . kept hoping so that today I wake up every morning in a house that was built by slaves."* Michelle Obama ended her speech declaring triumphantly—in a clear rebuke to Donald Trump—"Don't let anyone ever tell you that this country isn't great, that somehow we need to make it great again. Because this right now is the greatest country on earth." But the actual state of the country has never been measured or determined by the wealthiest and most powerful—even in those few instances when those people are Black or Brown. A more accurate view of the United States comes from the ground, not the perch of the White House. When we judge this country by the life of Charleena Lyles, a thirty-year-old, single Black mother, who was shot seven times and killed by Seattle police officers in June 2017, the picture comes into sharper focus.† The ability to distinguish between the ideology of the American Dream and the experience of the American nightmare requires political analysis, history, and often

---

* "Transcript: Read Michelle Obama's Full Speech from the 2016 DNC," *Washington Post*, July 26, 2016, https://www.washingtonpost.com/news/post-politics/wp/2016/07/26/transcript-read-michelle-obamas-full-speech-from-the-2016-dnc/.

† Christine Clarridge, "Autopsy Shows Charleena Lyles Was Shot Seven Times by Police," *Seattle Times*, August 30, 2017, www.seattletimes.com/seattle-news/autopsy-shows-charleena-lyles-was-shot-7-times-by-police/.

struggle. The Combahee River Collective employed this dynamic approach to politics, not a reductive analysis that implied identity alone was enough to overcome the sharp differences imposed by social class in our society.*

The women of the CRC did not define "identity politics" as exclusionary, whereby only those experiencing a particular oppression could fight against it. Nor did they envision identity politics as a tool to claim the mantle of "most oppressed." They saw it as an analysis that would validate Black women's experiences while simultaneously creating an opportunity for them to become politically active to fight for the issues most important to them.

To that end, the CRC Statement was clear in its calls for solidarity as the only way for Black women to win their struggles. Solidarity did not mean subsuming your struggles to help someone else; it was intended to strengthen the political commitments from other groups by getting them to recognize how the different struggles were related to each other and connected under capitalism. It called for greater awareness and understanding, not less. The CRC referred to this kind of approach to activism as coalition building, and they saw it as key to winning their struggles. Their analysis, "If Black women were free, it would mean that everyone else would have to be free since our freedom would necessitate the destruction of all the systems of oppression," captures the dialectic connecting the struggle for Black liberation to the struggle for a liberated United States and, ultimately, the world.

Finally, the CRC was important because of its internationalism. Before the multicultural moniker "women of color," there were "third world women." The distinction was important histori-

---

* Joy James, "Radicalizing Feminism," in *The Black Feminist Reader*, edited by Joy James and T. Denean Sharpley-Whiting (Hoboken, NJ: John Wiley & Sons, 2000).

cally as well as politically. It was a way of demonstrating solidarity with women in countries that were often suffering because of the policies and military actions of the US government. It was also a way of identifying with various anticolonial struggles and national liberation movements around the world. But of even more importance was the way that Black women saw themselves not as isolated within the United States but as part of a global movement of Black and Brown people united in struggle against the colonial, imperialist, and capitalist domination of the West, led by the United States. One can see the importance of international solidarity and identification especially today, when the United States so readily uses the abuse of women in other countries, such as Afghanistan, as a pretext for military intervention.

The women of Combahee tied their sophisticated political analysis to a "clear leap into revolutionary action." For them, the recognition of oppression was not enough; analysis was a guide to action and political activity. This is why this forty-year-old document remains so important. The plight and exploitation of Black women has continued into the twenty-first century, and it is paralleled by growing misery across the United States. The concentration of wealth and power among the "1 percent" is matched only by the growing poverty and deprivation of the bottom 99 percent. Of course, those experiences are not shared equally, as Black women and men are overrepresented in the most dismal categories used to measure the quality of life in the United States. But it does mean that those whom capitalism materially benefits are decidedly small in number, while those with mutual interest in creating a society based on human need are broad and expansive. There are, of course, many obstacles to achieving the kind of consciousness combined with political action necessary to make such a society a possibility. But the CRC Statement offers an analysis and a plan for "revolutionary action" that is not limited by time and distance from the circumstances in which the members wrote it. Their anticapitalism, calls for solidarity, and commitment to the radical idea that another world is possible and, indeed, necessary remain relevant.

This small book, *How We Get Free—Black Feminism and the Combahee River Collective*, is an effort to reconnect the radical roots of Black feminist analysis and practice to contemporary organizing efforts. In the same ways that Marxism became a tool for critical analysis in the academy of the 1980s and 1990s, so too did Black feminism find a home in academic circles as the political movements that engendered its rise began to recede from the streets. CRC coauthor Barbara Smith is credited as a founder of Black women's studies. This was critical in opening up spaces for intellectual inquiry and deeper investigation into the lives of the oppressed within the academy more generally. But Black feminism is a guide to political action and liberation. Political analysis outside of political movements and struggles becomes abstract, discourse driven, and disconnected from the radicalism that made it powerful in the first place.

In the last several years, Black feminism has reemerged as the analytical framework for the activist response to the oppression of trans women of color, the fight for reproductive rights, and, of course, the movement against police abuse and violence. The most visible organizations and activists connected to the Black Lives Matter movement speak openly about how Black feminism shapes their politics and strategies today. The interviews I have compiled in this book—with the three authors of the Combahee River Collective Statement, Barbara Smith, Beverly Smith, and Demita Frazier, #BlackLivesMatter cofounder Alicia Garza, and historian and activist Barbara Ransby—are an attempt to show how these politics remain historically vibrant and relevant to the struggles of today. As Demita Frazier says, the point of talking about Combahee is not to be nostalgic; rather, we talk about it because Black women are still not free.

THE COMBAHEE RIVER COLLECTIVE STATEMENT

We are a collective of Black feminists who have been meeting together since 1974. During that time we have been involved in the process of defining and clarifying our politics, while at the same time doing political work within our own group and in coalition with other progressive organizations and movements. The most general statement of our politics at the present time would be that we are actively committed to struggling against racial, sexual, heterosexual, and class oppression, and see as our particular task the development of integrated analysis and practice based upon the fact that the major systems of oppression are interlocking. The synthesis of these oppressions creates the conditions of our lives. As Black women we see Black feminism as the logical political movement to combat the manifold and simultaneous oppressions that all women of color face.

We will discuss four major topics in the paper that follows: (1) the genesis of contemporary Black feminism; (2) what we believe, i.e., the specific province of our politics; (3) the problems in organizing Black feminists, including a brief herstory of our collective; and (4) Black feminist issues and practice.

1. The Genesis of Contemporary Black Feminism

Before looking at the recent development of Black feminism we would like to affirm that we find our origins in the historical reality of Afro-American women's continuous life-and-death struggle for survival and liberation. Black women's extremely negative relationship to the American political system (a system of white male rule) has always been determined by our membership in two oppressed racial and sexual castes. As Angela Davis points out in "Reflections on the Black Woman's Role in the Community of Slaves," Black women have always embodied, if only in their physical manifestation, an adversary stance to white male rule and have actively resisted its inroads upon them and their communities in both dramatic and subtle ways. There have always been Black women activists—some known, like Sojourner Truth, Harriet Tubman, Frances E. W. Harper, Ida B. Wells Barnett, and Mary Church Terrell, and thousands upon thousands unknown—who have had a shared awareness of how their sexual identity combined with their racial identity to make their whole life situation and the focus of their political struggles unique. Contemporary Black feminism is the outgrowth of countless generations of personal sacrifice, militancy, and work by our mothers and sisters.

A Black feminist presence has evolved most obviously in connection with the second wave of the American women's movement beginning in the late 1960s. Black, other Third World, and working women have been involved in the feminist movement from its start, but both outside reactionary forces and racism and elitism within the movement itself have served to obscure our participation. In 1973, Black feminists, primarily located in New York, felt the necessity of forming a separate Black feminist group. This became the National Black Feminist Organization (NBFO).

Black feminist politics also have an obvious connection to movements for Black liberation, particularly those of the 1960s and 1970s. Many of us were active in those movements (Civil Rights, Black nationalism, the Black Panthers), and all of our lives were greatly affected and changed by their ideologies, their goals, and the tactics used to achieve their goals. It was our experience and disillusionment within these liberation movements, as well as experience on the periphery of the white male left, that led to the need to develop a politics that was antiracist, unlike those of white women, and antisexist, unlike those of Black and white men.

There is also undeniably a personal genesis for Black feminism, that is, the political realization that comes from the seemingly personal experiences of individual Black women's lives. Black feminists and many more Black women who do not define themselves as feminists have all experienced sexual oppression as a constant factor in our day-to-day existence. As children we realized that we were different from boys and that we were treated differently. For example, we were told in the same breath to be quiet both for the sake of being "ladylike" and to make us less objectionable in the eyes of white people. As we grew older we became aware of the threat of physical and sexual abuse by men. However, we had no way of conceptualizing what was so apparent to us, what we knew was really happening.

Black feminists often talk about their feelings of craziness before becoming conscious of the concepts of sexual politics, patriarchal rule, and most importantly, feminism, the political analysis and practice that we women use to struggle against our oppression. The fact that racial politics and indeed racism are pervasive factors in our lives did not allow us, and still does not allow most Black women, to look more deeply into our own experiences and, from that sharing and growing consciousness, to build a politics that will change our lives and inevitably end our oppression. Our development must also be tied to the contemporary economic and political position of Black people. The post–World War II generation of Black youth was the first to be able to minimally partake of certain educational and employment options, previously closed completely to Black people. Although our economic position is still at the very bottom of the American capitalistic economy, a handful of us have been able to gain certain tools as a result of tokenism in education and employment which potentially enable us to more effectively fight our oppression.

A combined antiracist and antisexist position drew us together initially, and as we developed politically we addressed ourselves to heterosexism and economic oppression under capitalism.

2. What We Believe

Above all else, our politics initially sprang from the shared belief that Black women are inherently valuable, that our liberation is a necessity not as an adjunct to somebody else's but because of our need as human persons for autonomy. This may seem so obvious as to sound simplistic, but it is apparent that no other ostensibly progressive movement has ever considered our specific oppression as a priority or worked seriously for the ending of that oppression. Merely naming the pejorative stereotypes attributed to Black women (e.g., mammy, matriarch, Sapphire, whore, bulldagger), let alone cataloguing the cruel, often murderous, treatment we receive, indicates how little value has been placed upon our lives during four centuries of bondage in the Western Hemisphere. We realize that the only people who care enough about us to work consistently for our liberation are us. Our politics evolve from a healthy love for ourselves, our sisters and our community which allows us to continue our struggle and work.

This focusing upon our own oppression is embodied in the concept of identity politics. We believe that the most profound and potentially most radical politics come directly out of our own identity, as opposed to working to end somebody else's oppression. In the case of Black women this is a particularly repugnant, dangerous, threatening, and therefore revolutionary concept because it is obvious from looking at all the political movements that have preceded us that anyone is more worthy of liberation than ourselves. We reject pedestals, queenhood, and walking ten paces behind. To be recognized as human, levelly human, is enough.

We believe that sexual politics under patriarchy is as pervasive in Black women's lives as are the politics of class and race. We also often find it difficult to separate race from class from sex oppression because in our lives they are most often experienced simultaneously. We know that there is such a thing as racial-sexual oppression which is neither solely racial nor solely sexual, e.g., the history of rape of Black women by white men as a weapon of political repression.

Although we are feminists and lesbians, we feel solidarity with progressive Black men and do not advocate the fractionalization that white women who are separatists demand. Our situation as Black people necessitates that we have solidarity around the fact of race, which white women of course do not need to have with white men, unless it is their negative solidarity as racial oppressors. We struggle together with Black men against racism, while we also struggle with Black men about sexism.

We realize that the liberation of all oppressed peoples necessitates the destruction of the political-economic systems of capitalism and imperialism as well as patriarchy. We are socialists because we believe that work must be organized for the collective benefit of those who do the work and create the products, and not for the profit of the bosses. Material resources must be equally distributed among those who create these resources. We are not convinced, however, that a socialist revolution that is not also a feminist and antiracist revolution will guarantee our liberation. We have arrived at the necessity for developing an understanding of class relationships that takes into account the specific class position of Black women who are generally marginal in the labor force, while at this particular time some of us are temporarily viewed as doubly desirable tokens at white-collar and professional levels. We need to articulate the real class situation of persons who are not merely raceless, sexless workers, but for whom racial and sexual oppression are significant determinants in their working/economic lives. Although we are in essential agreement with Marx's theory as it applied to the very specific economic relationships he analyzed, we know that his analysis must be extended further in order for us to understand our specific economic situation as Black women.

A political contribution which we feel we have already made is the expansion of the feminist principle that the personal is political. In our consciousness-raising sessions, for example, we have in many ways gone beyond white women's revelations because we are dealing with the implications of race and class as well as sex. Even our Black women's style of talking/testifying in Black language about what we have experienced has a resonance that is both cultural and political. We have spent a great deal of energy delving into the cultural and experiential nature of our oppression out of necessity because none of these matters has ever been looked at before. No one before has ever examined the multilayered texture of Black women's lives. An example of this kind of revelation/conceptualization occurred at a meeting as we discussed the ways in which our early intellectual interests had been attacked by our peers, particularly Black males. We discovered that all of us, because we were "smart," had also been considered "ugly," i.e., "smart-ugly." "Smart-ugly" crystallized the way in which most of us had been forced to develop our intellects at great cost to our "social" lives. The sanctions in the Black and white communities against Black women thinkers [are] comparatively much higher than for white women, particularly ones from the educated middle and upper classes.

As we have already stated, we reject the stance of lesbian separatism because it is not a viable political analysis or strategy for us. It leaves out far too much and far too many people, particularly Black men, women, and children. We have a great deal of criticism and loathing for what men have been socialized to be in this society: what they support, how they act, and how they oppress. But we do not have the misguided notion that it is their maleness, per se—i.e., their biological maleness—that makes them what they are. As Black women we find any type of biological determinism a particularly dangerous and reactionary basis upon which to build a politic. We must also question whether lesbian separatism is an adequate and progressive political analysis and strategy, even for those who practice it, since it so completely denies any but the sexual sources of women's oppression, negating the facts of class and race.

3. Problems in Organizing Black Feminists

During our years together as a Black feminist collective we have experienced success and defeat, joy and pain, victory and failure. We have found that it is very difficult to organize around Black feminist issues, difficult even to announce in certain contexts that we are Black feminists. We have tried to think about the reasons for our difficulties, particularly since the white women's movement continues to be strong and to grow in many directions. In this section we will discuss some of the general reasons for the organizing problems we face and also talk specifically about the stages in organizing our own collective.

The major source of difficulty in our political work is that we are not just trying to fight oppression on one front or even two, but instead to address a whole range of oppressions. We do not have racial, sexual, heterosexual, or class privilege to rely upon, nor do we have even the minimal access to resources and power that groups who possess any one of these types of privilege have.

The psychological toll of being a Black woman and the difficulties this presents in reaching political consciousness and doing political work can never be underestimated. There is a very low value placed upon Black women's psyches in this society, which is both racist and sexist. As an early group member once said, "We are all damaged people merely by virtue of being Black women." We are dispossessed psychologically and on every other level, and yet we feel the necessity to struggle to change the condition of all Black women. In "A Black Feminist's Search for Sisterhood," Michele Wallace arrives at this conclusion: "We exist as women who are Black who are feminists, each stranded for the moment, working independently because there is not yet an environment in this society remotely congenial to our struggle—because, being on the bottom, we would have to do what no one else has done: we would have to fight the world."[*]

Wallace is pessimistic but realistic in her assessment of Black feminists' position, particularly in her allusion to the nearly classic isolation most of us face. We might use our position at the bottom, however, to make a clear leap into revolutionary action. If Black

---

[*] Michele Wallace, "A Black Feminist's Search for Sisterhood," *Village Voice*, July 28, 1975, 6–7.

women were free, it would mean that everyone else would have to be free since our freedom would necessitate the destruction of all the systems of oppression.

Feminism is, nevertheless, very threatening to the majority of Black people because it calls into question some of the most basic assumptions about our existence, i.e., that sex should be a determinant of power relationships. Here is the way male and female roles were defined in a Black nationalist pamphlet from the early 1970s:

> We understand that it is and has been traditional that the man is the head of the house. He is the leader of the house/nation because his knowledge of the world is broader, his awareness is greater, his understanding is fuller and his application of this information is wiser. . . . After all, it is only reasonable that the man be the head of the house because he is able to defend and protect the development of his home . . . Women cannot do the same things as men—they are made by nature to function differently. Equality of men and women is something that cannot happen even in the abstract world. Men are not equal to other men, i.e., ability, experience or even understanding. The value of men and women can be seen as in the value of gold and silver—they are not equal but both have great value. We must realize that men and women are a complement to each other because there is no house/family without a man and his wife. Both are essential to the development of any life.*

The material conditions of most Black women would hardly lead them to upset both economic and sexual arrangements that seem to represent some stability in their lives. Many Black women have a good understanding of both sexism and racism, but, because of the everyday constrictions of their lives, cannot risk struggling against them both.

---

* Mumininas of Committee for Unified Newark, *Mwanamke Mwananchi* (The Nationalist Woman) (Newark, NJ: Mumininas of CUN, 1971), 4–5.

The reaction of Black men to feminism has been notoriously negative. They are, of course, even more threatened than Black women by the possibility that Black feminists might organize around our own needs. They realize that they might not only lose valuable and hardworking allies in their struggles but that they might also be forced to change their habitually sexist ways of interacting with and oppressing Black women. Accusations that Black feminism divides the Black struggle are powerful deterrents to the growth of an autonomous Black women's movement.

Still, hundreds of women have been active at different times during the three-year existence of our group. And every Black woman who came, came out of a strongly felt need for some level of possibility that did not previously exist in her life.

When we first started meeting early in 1974 after the NBFO first eastern regional conference, we did not have a strategy for organizing, or even a focus. We just wanted to see what we had. After a period of months of not meeting, we began to meet again late in the year and started doing an intense variety of consciousness-raising. The overwhelming feeling that we had is that after years and years we had finally found each other. Although we were not doing political work as a group, individuals continued their involvement in lesbian politics, sterilization abuse and abortion rights work, Third World Women's International Women's Day activities, and support activity for the trials of Dr. Kenneth Edelin, Joan Little, and Inéz García. During our first summer when membership had dropped off considerably, those of us remaining devoted serious discussion to the possibility of opening a refuge for battered women in a Black community. (There was no refuge in Boston at that time.) We also decided around that time to become an independent collective since we had serious disagreements with NBFO's bourgeois-feminist stance and their lack of a clear political focus.

We also were contacted at that time by socialist feminists, with whom we had worked on abortion rights activities, who wanted to encourage us to attend the National Socialist Feminist Conference in Yellow Springs. One of our members did attend and, despite the narrowness of the ideology that was promoted at that particular conference, we became more aware of the need for us to understand our own economic situation and to make our own economic analysis.

In the fall, when some members returned, we experienced several months of comparative inactivity and internal disagreements, which were first conceptualized as a lesbian-straight split but which were also the result of class and political differences. During the summer those of us who were still meeting had determined the need to do political work and to move beyond consciousness-raising and serving exclusively as an emotional support group. At the beginning of 1976, when some of the women who had not wanted to do political work and who also had voiced disagreements stopped attending of their own accord, we again looked for a focus. We decided at that time, with the addition of new members, to become a study group. We had always shared our reading with each other, and some of us had written papers on Black feminism for group discussion a few months before this decision was made. We began functioning as a study group and also began discussing the possibility of starting a Black feminist publication. We had a retreat in the late spring which provided a time for both political discussion and working out interpersonal issues. Currently we are planning to gather together a collection of Black feminist writing. We feel that it is absolutely essential to demonstrate the reality of our politics to other Black women and believe that we can do this through writing and distributing our work. The fact that individual Black feminists are living in isolation all over the country, that our own numbers are small, and that we have some skills in writing, printing, and publishing makes us want to carry out these kinds of projects as a means of organizing Black feminists as we continue to do political work in coalition with other groups.

4. Black Feminist Issues and Projects

During our time together we have identified and worked on many issues of particular relevance to Black women. The inclusiveness of our politics makes us concerned with any situation that impinges upon the lives of women, Third World and working people. We are of course particularly committed to working on those struggles in which race, sex, and class are simultaneous factors in oppression. We might, for example, become involved in workplace organizing at a factory that employs Third World women or picket a hospital that is cutting back on already inadequate health care to a Third World community, or set up a rape crisis center in a Black neighborhood. Organizing around welfare and daycare concerns might also be a focus. The work to be done and the countless issues that this work represents merely reflect the pervasiveness of our oppression.

Issues and projects that collective members have actually worked on are sterilization abuse, abortion rights, battered women, rape and health care. We have also done many workshops and educationals on Black feminism on college campuses, at women's conferences, and most recently for high school women.

One issue that is of major concern to us and that we have begun to publicly address is racism in the white women's movement. As Black feminists we are made constantly and painfully aware of how little effort white women have made to understand and combat their racism, which requires among other things that they have a more than superficial comprehension of race, color, and Black history and culture. Eliminating racism in the white women's movement is by definition work for white women to do, but we will continue to speak to and demand accountability on this issue.

In the practice of our politics we do not believe that the end always justifies the means. Many reactionary and destructive acts have been done in the name of achieving "correct" political goals. As feminists we do not want to mess over people in the name of politics. We believe in collective process and a nonhierarchical distribution of power within our own group and in our vision of a revolutionary society. We are committed to a continual examination of our politics as they develop through criticism and self-criticism as an essential aspect of our practice. In her introduction to *Sisterhood is Powerful* Robin Morgan writes: "I haven't the faintest notion what possible revolutionary role white heterosexual men could fulfill, since they are the very embodiment of reactionary-vested-interest-power."

As Black feminists and lesbians we know that we have a very definite revolutionary task to perform and we are ready for the lifetime of work and struggle before us.

Combahee River Collective, April 1977

BARBARA SMITH

KEEANGA-YAMAHTTA TAYLOR: It's the fortieth anniversary of the publication of the Combahee River Collective Statement. First, how do you pronounce it?

BARBARA SMITH: We always said *Comm-buh-hee*. Some people say *comb*—like, you know, a comb that you comb your hair with . . . I don't know what the real pronunciation is. I have visited there [the Combahee River area in South Carolina], and I think I was around people who pronounced it correctly, and I can't tell you exactly if it matched my pronunciation or if it was something slightly different. But I would say *Comm-buh-hee*, like the beginning of Comcast or something.

Well, why don't you tell me where the name comes from— what inspired the collective that formed?

I don't know if this is in the Combahee River Collective Statement itself or if it's in commentary that I have done. One of the things that was happening during that time—pretty much the beginning of the second wave of the feminist moment—was that white women were, for lack of a better word, well, I'll just say *taking* instead of appropriating. They were taking the names of Black women, particularly Harriet Tubman and Sojourner Truth, and using them for different projects. There was a longtime feminist newspaper in Boston, which evolved over the years into an excellent feminist newspaper. Its name was *Sojourner*. Are you familiar with that one?

Yes.

So there was *Sojourner*. I can't remember if there was anything specifically focused upon Harriet Tubman, except that there was a social service agency in the South End of Boston, which was one of the poor working-class and lower-middle-class sections of Boston—at least in the 1970s it was. It was gentrifying and now it's unrecognizable as what I just described. But, as I said, there was a settlement house in the South End called the Harriet Tubman House, and then they built a new building. Harriet Tubman House was on our radar, although I think we decided to name ourselves the Combahee River Collective before that new building for Harriet Tubman House actually opened.

I had read that short biography, from I think International Publishers, about Harriet Tubman. I don't know if International Publishers still publishes, but they were definitely a leftist press. And it was a very short biography, like maybe about fifty or sixty pages, but full of information that you would not necessarily get elsewhere. And it talked about her having planned and led this raid on the Combahee River that freed over 750 people who were enslaved.

So when we were talking about becoming independent and what to name ourselves, I suggested Combahee. Some of the other members probably read the book, borrowed the book—I told them about what had happened at the Combahee River. So we all agreed we wanted to be the Combahee River Collective. My perspective, and I think it was shared, was let's not name ourselves after a person. Let's name ourselves after an action.

A political action. And that's what we did. And not only a political action but a political action for liberation.

Absolutely.

Harriet Tubman—and I think this would be true until this day—as you know, was a scout for the Union Army, and hers was the first and only military campaign in US history that was planned and led by a woman. Yeah, and I know there are generals—women generals now. So I don't know exactly how that fits in with what they have done in our continuing imperialist adventures [laugh] around the globe.

When did you become a feminist?

I began to identify or to be curious about feminism in the early 1970s. I graduated from college in 1969. I was very involved in political organizing on my campus, which was Mount Holyoke, including being involved in the peace movement to end the war in Vietnam. And that was stepping out there for a Black woman, although there were some other Black women who were also involved. There were a tiny, tiny number of Black women on that campus anyway.

There were not that many Black women or Black men involved in the movement to end the war in Vietnam. There just weren't that many. We finally took heart when Martin Luther King spoke out about the war. And that was during my college years. I was involved in a group called the Civil Action Group. They had focused on civil rights issues. But by the time I got to college in '65, the civil rights movement was really changing, and morphing, into Black liberation, Black power, and Black nationalism. I was also involved in student organizing around campus issues, particularly Black student organizing.

I spent my junior year at the New School for Social Research. There was a college program that they had just started, and it was a two-year college program for juniors and seniors only. So they really had designed it to pull people transferring from other institutions. And because of the content and the perspective of the New School College, and also the context of the New School for Social Research, which of course has always been at least a progressive academic institution, they were really pulling students who were some of the most dissident in the entire nation. Because they were all students who were not satisfied with where they were.

I had transferred from Mount Holyoke, which was a pretty conservative middle-of-the-road institution in many ways, but there were students in my program from Antioch, from Reed, maybe even UC Berkeley, et cetera. So the first day [laughter] we had this assembly—and it was of course a small group of students, like a hundred or so perhaps—but the first time we had a meeting in the beginning of the semester—this was the fall of '67—I looked around this auditorium and I thought, "Wow, these are some of the most dissident students in the entire country! And I'm with them!" You know? [laugh]

So that was great, because I was already radicalized in some senses. But being at the New School, I became even more so, because there were people in my classes who were very involved in SDS—Students for a Democratic Society. Our teachers were also young radicals, by and large. So it was a wonderful experience for me. I came back to Mount Holyoke then my senior year. But in the meantime, the summer of '68, I had been in Chicago for the Chicago convention demonstrations . . . against the war.

Were you participating in the Democratic National Convention protests? What brought you there?

Oh yeah, that's why I went.

Who did you go with?

I went to participate in the protests. I certainly didn't go to participate in the damn convention! [laugh] I have never been—even though I was an elected Democrat twice, in the city of Albany, I've never been immersed in Democratic Party politics. I mean, it's just not anything that I would ever have been involved with. Sixty-eight was the first presidential election that I could vote in. And whoever was the Black Panther—I want to say it was Bobby Seale—who ran for president that year, that's who I voted for. So that was my first presidential election!

I went with a couple of guys I had met. I had a job the summer of '68 at what was then Western Reserve University. It didn't become Case Western until some time later. [Case Institute of Technology was a separate institution.] So anyway, I was working as a dorm person responsible for a group of Upward Bound students,* as was one of the guys I went with to Chicago. I also ended up "teaching," and I'll put *teaching* in quotes, although I think I was probably quite capable of teaching during those years, even though I was still in college. I ended up teaching a course with another person who had a counterpart position with Upward Bound—a Black man who wanted to teach Black history. But his version of Black history and mine were totally different. Because he was basically teaching Black propaganda, and I was very interested in actually teaching African American history.

---

* Upward Bound was a college-prep program for low-income Black and Brown youth that was originally funded by the War on Poverty.

So we definitely knocked heads. He was very ideological and very sexist. But be that as it may, that's what I was doing. So one of the people I met was this wonderful guy named Allen Binstock, and he was a student at Western Reserve. He and another friend of his, and probably more friends who I do not recall—we clicked because we were activists and we were involved in the movement against the war in Vietnam. I think Allen might have been in SDS, probably.

We didn't have SDS at Mount Holyoke. I did not join SDS when I was at the New School because it was basically a white male organization. And I didn't really see myself—even though my politics were aligned with SDS, I just didn't see myself being in a white male–dominated organization. I met women—there were women who I knew when I was at the New School—I don't know if any of them were in SDS or not.

On what basis were your politics aligned? What were you in agreement with?

As I said, our politics were aligned. So Allen and some of his friends, all summer long, we were talking about the Chicago convention demonstrations, and wondering whether we were going to go because the Chicago police had let everybody know that they were about [laughter] beating heads. And being very, very adversarial if indeed people did come. And Rennie Davis, one of the leaders in SDS—he came and spoke, I believe, at Western Reserve—not connected to our Upward Bound program, but he came and spoke that summer. And after seeing Rennie speak, I was like, "Okay, I'm going. I'm going to do this."

The thing that I was going to say about my dear Aunt LaRue is that as my sister and I got more politically active—and we did get involved in the civil rights movement as teenagers in Cleveland—

she never put up any roadblocks. And I can only imagine—I can't tell you what was said when I told her—I don't know what she said to me when I said, "I want to go to Chicago for this anti–Vietnam War demonstration." Whatever she said, I don't remember it being a big fight. I mean, I don't remember any fight or conflict at all. Whatever was said, I went. She did not stand in the way.

And she and my sister—they were watching it on television as the police riot unfolded. And when I hear—sometimes you know on NPR or on the news, sometimes they'll do a story on the anniversary of the Chicago convention demonstrations. I swear, when I either hear a story or see a story like that, my anxiety just goes through the roof and I think, "I can't believe I was there. I can't believe I was there." So incredibly upsetting. And then I think about what my aunt and my sister were going through watching it on TV wondering they were ever going to see me again.

Right.

But as I said, I was given that amount of latitude, and of course this is a transforming experience. Now to get back to feminism in my senior year—the Columbia University strike happened during the year I was at the New School. So the New School closed down in solidarity with what was going on at Columbia. That's how hip the professors and the administration were at the New School. Its like, "Oh? Columbia's going out on strike? Okay, so we're closing down, so if you want to participate up there, go ahead."

So that's where I first got to read Marx and other socialist thinkers in the original. It was a great experience for me. Mark Rudd was speaking on one of the other nearby campuses—probably Amherst, in the early fall of 1968. So we go to see him, and then another friend of mine and I who I had just met—even though we were in the same class, we connected because she also had been in Chicago for the demonstration. We bonded around that. And I think it was Betsy who said, "We've got to bring Mark Rudd to Mount Holyoke!" [laugh] And you know, better to ask forgiveness than to ask permission. That's how we operated.

He said he would come, and we had this beautiful outdoor amphitheater at Mount Holyoke. It was a gorgeous fall day. I had really good relationships with the people who ran what was called our Fellowship of Faiths. We did not have a student union or anything like that, but our Fellowship of Faiths functioned in many ways like a student center because you could do things there—have meetings, bake. You know, or cook meals—there was a kitchen, et cetera.

The dean of the college chapel and the assistant dean of the college chapel—they were people who I had had really good relationships with during my first two years at Mount Holyoke. We asked them if they would provide the sound system, which they did. And the way that we advertised that Mark Rudd was going to be there was that we wrote in colored chalk on the sidewalks [laugh] "Mark Rudd, today, amphitheater, 12 o'clock." That's what we did.

My understanding is that the administration was losing their natural minds. They were losing their minds, because Mark Rudd, well-known student radical, male [laugh] from Columbia, is going to be at Mount Holyoke. And what can we do? They did not stop us. I mean, they could have. I think that the police were certainly made aware that this was happening. But he did come, and he did speak. So, when did I first get involved with feminism? He was traveling with a woman in her early twenties, in our age group, who described herself as being a part of women's liberation.

And I looked at this white woman and I could not even understand—what the hell is she talking about? I could not—this is '68, right? I had no idea what she was talking about, because she was white, you know? And my perspective was, like many Black women—and even now some Black women still hold this today—my perspective then was like, "What do white women have to complain about? I mean, they've been terrorizing us in their homes and in their kitchens for several centuries here now." "They are the excuse for a pandemic of lynchings in the United States." Their status as, you know, "pure white women" is instrumental, and has been instrumental, in lynching and other forms of racial violence. Their status also was the absolute opposite of what our status was as Black women. So I couldn't even wrap my mind around it.

But after I got out of college and began to deal with not so much the workforce—though that to some extent, because I went directly from college to grad school—but trying to do things, to buy a portable electric typewriter as I started my graduate work at the University of Pittsburgh—I couldn't get one. I could not put it on credit or anything—because I couldn't apply for credit in my own name on my own behalf because I was female!

Wow.

Now a young male recent college graduate—I mean, and mark my words, college graduate, right? That guy would have been able to get credit. But you couldn't get credit in those days unless it was attached to your husband! I mean, that's in my own lifetime! How insane is this, you know? So I said to my dear Aunt LaRue, "I need to get an electric typewriter." I had a manual. I said, "I really need to get an electric typewriter." I said, "Would you get it for me and I'll pay you back?" And that's exactly how I got that typewriter. Which is ridiculous.

During the spring of my senior year [when I was home for break]—because I always like to try to keep options open if I can—I thought, "Well, let me go and explore perhaps working for an airline." Because one of my big, big, dreams as a young person was to travel. That was really high on my list. We didn't travel when I was growing up, probably much to our benefit, given that it was during Jim Crow [laugh]. We didn't have the [financial] wherewithal to travel, and we also did not go down south where all our family came from. That was Georgia. We didn't make the trip that many of our peers were making during that time. And I'm glad that we didn't because I think my sister and I, I think our spirits would have been completely crushed. Anyway, I went to Pan Am—Pan American had an office downtown, as did other airlines. And I went to have a job interview at Pan American because I thought, yeah, that will get me a few places, you know?

In those days there were downtown ticket offices. And these offices were not big. But there was a young white man who was the person doing the interview. I took the test, and I completely aced the test, you know. [laugh] So he had that usual deer in the headlights expression, *How did you possibly get this kind of grade on this test given that you're not white and male?* But I took the test and I was talking to him about the possible career options—it would have meant relocating to Chicago because that's where one of their headquarters was. I did not have any desire to fly as a part of my job. We talked about me being a reservationist, and I said to him—I had enough sense to say to him, even as a not-quite-graduated senior in 1969, I said, "And what would be the possibilities for management or career advancement?" He told me that there would be none.

Because I was female! And I said to myself, "You know what? I'm going to go to grad school!" [laugh]

Right, right.

And these are things that were happening to me in real time. Also, I was trying to be a heterosexual at that time. And there were certain kinds of expectations around what I was supposed to be interested in and doing versus what the males were doing—you know, we socialized with other couples, and one of the things that used to interest me is that when the women were in the kitchen, I'd be out there in the living room, talking to the guys. Because I was interested in ideas, et cetera.

There were all these what used to be called *clicks*—you know, as in a click, like a light bulb—a lamp clicking on, and you'd say, "Oh! Oh, Okay." "Oh! So that's what's going on in relationship to sexism and gender roles!" After I finished my masters at the University of Pittsburgh, I was at the University of Connecticut working on my doctorate, and I got a job working at Phillips Academy in Andover, which as you know, is one of the bastions of white male elite privilege in this nation.

That's where I met the guy who I was talking about—I ended up socializing with other couples with him in Boston, because he lived in Boston. And one of the things that happened that summer is that *Ms.* magazine published its first issue. I was a charter subscriber to *Ms.*, and also I got a copy of *Our Bodies, Ourselves* during that time period too. I was alert to and interested in feminism. I can't remember what year it was, but it was in the early '70s. I think I was still at the University of Pittsburgh, so very early '70s. I got my master's in '71. And one of my other aunts gave me a gift certificate to a local bookstore, and what did I go and buy with my gift certificate? Kate Millett's *Sexual Politics*. So I was interested in it.

My first semester at UConn I'm taking this course then in women's literature, and we started with—there's a woman named Aphra Behn, I assume British—and she was writing probably in the 1600s —it was a long time ago. We started that far back. She's known for being one of the first, if not the first, published women writers during that period. I talked to my professor and I said, "I want to do my seminar paper on a Black woman writer." And she had nothing to tell me. I had already done an independent study at Mount Holyoke on four major Black writers, including Wright, Baldwin, Ellison, Amiri Baraka, who at that time was still LeRoi Jones. So I had already done that, you know? It's not like I wasn't trying to teach myself the discipline. But it didn't occur to me at that point that I could include a woman writer, and I didn't even know any major Black women writers to include. But when I talked to my seminar professor, she didn't have any suggestions for me. I think she let me borrow a copy of Gerda Lerner's book, *Black Women in White America: A Documentary History.* All well and good—I loved the book. But it wasn't a book that collected literary—creative literature by Black women writers. Then my aunt died suddenly . . . in late 1971, in November. I took incompletes in the courses I was taking at that time. And then I read in one of the early issues of *Ms.* magazine that Alice Walker, who I was already familiar with—nobody else knew who she was, but I did, because I read everything. I had seen poetry by her in *Harper's* magazine, actually. So I read that she was in the Boston area, up from Mississippi, and she was going to be teaching a course on Black women writers.

I said, "Wow!" I was so excited. And she would be doing that at Wellesley. I wrote to her and I asked if I could audit her course. By the time I connected with her, because she taught it a second time, she was teaching at UMass Boston, the downtown campus, not the Columbia Point campus, because I don't think they had even finished building the Columbia Point campus at that point. But anyway, they had different colleges—colleges 1, 2, and 3—at UMass Boston at that time. And college 3 was the one for adult learners, and it was, as I said, downtown, in these kind of ramshackle, not fancy, buildings.

But that's where I first got really exposed to Black women's literature. My sister in the meantime had gotten a job working at *Ms.* She lived in New York. She was married briefly during that period. And she met Margaret Sloan, who was one of the major founders of the National Black Feminist Organization. By the fall of '73, I was teaching at Emerson College, and I said, after having audited this course with Alice, "I don't know when my next teaching job will be." And I never really had had a teaching job that was not associated with a graduate fellowship or assistantship. But I said, "Wherever I teach, the next time I teach, I'm going to teach Black women writers." I asserted that as a goal.

And lo and behold, one year later, fall of '73, I got a job teaching at Emerson College. There was a wonderful woman who was chair of the English department, and besides the required composition courses that I had to teach, and African American literature—which, of course, I wanted to teach—she said, "Is there anything else? What other things would you like to teach?" I said, "Black women writers." She said, "Fine." [laugh]

So that was my first course. I'm teaching my first course on Black women writers. And then later that fall, the National Black Feminist Organization had its first Eastern Regional Conference, and that was the springboard for our starting an NBFO chapter in Boston, which eventually became Combahee. So I'm not capable of giving short answers.

Oh, no, this is fantastic. Will you say something about coming into contact with NBFO? What were some of the discussions surrounding the feminist movement at that time? Earlier you talked about second-wave feminism.

Right.

Now you're talking about the founding of this chapter in Boston. What were some of the debates animating feminism at this time?

Well, one of the debates was "How are you going to deal with race?" Does the feminist movement as a whole, does the women's movement as a whole have any racial consciousness or any interest in dealing with the racial politics and the racism and white supremacy of the nation in which it is indeed located? That was a big question. One of the things that enhanced concern about that question is that Boston at that time was in a state of racial warfare because of the court-ordered school desegregation and school busing. It was like World War III up in there! It was violent. It was frightening. And to say that the city was divided doesn't even begin to describe—[what it was like] to be a young Black woman living in that city, trying to do very different kinds of politics than the usual—in other words, Black feminist politics—and to be doing it in a context of, as I said, just outright racial warfare.

Brenda Verner, who was very antifeminist, came to our first NBFO meeting in Boston—and as a result there were some women who never came back. They never returned. That meeting was held in Roxbury, which as you know is the core Black community in Boston. In mid '74 I moved to Washington, DC, to work for a major national newspaper, the *National Observer*. I only stayed there for six months, but it was a good time to be in Washington, because that was the summer that Nixon got his behind on the plane—on the helicopter. So it was an interesting time to be working in media. The job wasn't working out because of the racism and the sexism. I came back to Boston in late '74. But in the meantime, Demita had written me a letter . . . and said she was really interested in our formulating and beginning to start a chapter of NBFO in Boston. The letter was forwarded from my Boston address. I explained to her that I wasn't in Boston at the time but that I would be returning soon. The thing I want you to keep in mind about the context of our organizing is that we were organizing in the context of a race war. They almost beat a Black man to death in Government Center, where the city hall is in Boston, using a staff of a flagpole to do it. Look it up. Ted Landsmark. He was dressed nicely in a three-piece suit. And he was a young Black lawyer.*

So, a major question was racial politics. And then the one that was right next to it was class and economic politics. We connected with socialist feminists in the Boston area during that period because they were the feminists who actually had a race and class analysis. Now whether they were completely woke—to use a contemporary term—who is, and are we ever? And that's when [Demita] and I met.

And there's so many things to say about Combahee. We need more dialogue about the history and the ongoing organizing of people who claim and share these politics. But there are a couple of things that I think are really important about why Combahee is still looked at as being valuable forty years later. And one is about why I think the work has continued to be relevant and useful. The other one is about the context of when and how we were doing our organizing. So the first is the fact that we were socialists. We were part of the organized left. We were not sectarian. We did not belong to

---

* Landsmark was a Yale-educated African American attorney. On the day he was attacked, he inadvertently landed in a rally of white students who opposed busing. Joseph Rakes was a white high school student and was wielding the American flag when he attacked Landsmark. Landsmark was taken to the hospital and suffered a broken nose as a result of the assault.

any parties or groups. Both Demita and I have never belonged to any party or organized formation. That's just where we were coming from. But we did consider ourselves to be a part of the left. We did consider ourselves to be socialist. And we had been involved in other radical struggles for justice prior to organizing something called a Black feminist collective. I had been involved in the movement to end the war in Vietnam, when I was in college. I was a few years older than Demita, so her high school years were my college years. And to be a Black woman involved in the antiwar movement at that time— that was not really anything that was easy—it was not easy to do. You faced the racism of the predominantly white antiwar movement, but you also experienced a lot of censure from the Black community and from Black activists who by that time in the early seventies had moved into Black nationalism and Black power. I was in grad school at the University of Pittsburgh during that period. They had one of the first Black studies departments in the nation. And I cannot tell you the amount of grief that I experienced because I actually thought that ending a war against people of color—that was fought predominantly by poor young men, who were disproportionately of color— was important. They thought that was irrelevant. That was a white thing to do. So as I said, we had paid—we had already paid some dues. And Demita [was] involved with the Panthers.

   One of the things about our involvement in the antiwar movement is something that characterized the politics of Combahee, which was our internationalism. This is not a part of our politics that has necessarily been uplifted widely, but that's where we were coming from. In those days, the term "women of color" or "people of color" was not used. It may have been used on the West Coast, but we were not there. I didn't hear it until the early eighties. We were third world women. We considered ourselves to be third world women. We saw ourselves in solidarity and in struggle with all third world people around the globe. And we also saw ourselves as being internally colonized. We were internally colonized within the United States. We identified as third world people. And that kind of solidarity was not just true of the very new Black feminism that we were building. Also at that time there was the gay rights movement—because that's what it was called, so I'm being historically accurate. What was then the gay rights movement—there was a part of the gay rights movement that also had that kind of solidarity and understanding that the "-isms" connected with each other. And that sector, if you haven't looked at that history, was in conflict many times with those who only wished to work on gay issues. You can see that Combahee had a very broad perspective.

I'm not saying that there were no kinds of tensions among and between us. There definitely were between us, as women of different racial and class backgrounds. But socialist feminists at least had it out on the table that they thought race and class were important oppressions to be integrated into an analysis of gender oppression. So we did a lot of work with socialist feminists, including me going to the socialist feminist conference that happened in Yellow Springs, Ohio, in the summer of '75. I can't remember if anybody else from Combahee went. But I met Cheryl Clarke there. She is a distinguished Black lesbian feminist poet and activist, and she was eventually published by Kitchen Table. You'll easily find her work. She still continues to publish new work. But I met Cheryl at the socialist feminist conference, and we were kind of like, "What in the hell are we doing here with all these white people?"

What was Kitchen Table Press and how did it come to be?

Kitchen Table: Women of Color Press was not a project of Combahee. Audre Lorde and I had become friends in the mid to late 1970s—she participated in our Black feminist Combahee River Collective retreats. And we also saw each other in other contexts, too. She was coming to Boston in the fall of 1980 to do a Black women's poetry reading on Halloween. Donna Kate Rushin, whose work is in both *Home Girls* and in *This Bridge Called My Back*—all of those books, of course, had not come out at that time. But Donna Kate Rushin, a wonderful writer and poet who lived in Boston. And I can't remember—there's a woman from New York—I think Hattie Gossett was also one of the people who was coming from New York to read. And then there was one other person, I think, from New York. But anyway, there was this wonderful white gay man who was really down with Black feminism and Black lesbians. His name was Clover Chango. And he was the organizer of this Black women's poetry reading. And he had done cultural events like that before, and would do things like that subsequently. So he was organizing this reading for Halloween in 1980. And Audre and I were talking on the phone prior to her coming for that purpose. And she said, "Barbara, we really need to do something about publishing." I don't know what preceded that remark. I don't know if we were talking about our most recent adventures with the white feminist publishing establishment, which was not really an establishment, but you know what I'm saying.

I'm referring to the infrastructure of the white feminist publishing movement, in which she and I were both thoroughly involved, both on the periodical side, and also on the press/publishing side, because our work was getting published in those places. When Audre said that, I said "Oh yes, definitely. We absolutely do." Because we had had some really not positive experiences dealing with white women publishers and publications. I said I would get together a meeting, during the time that she was in Boston, for that poetry reading on Halloween. We did have the meeting, and we had decided even from I think the beginning, because of who we invited to the meeting, that we would be a press for all women of color, not just for women of African heritage. There were some Latinas at the meeting. And that's how Kitchen Table began. And then we just continued to build and to organize. So it was not a project of Combahee. But it was the next thing after Combahee that I devoted a significant chunk of my life to.

Part of what you're saying is that, given some of the complications for women of color publishing with whatever number of white feminist presses existed at the time, that there was a particular role that could be played by Kitchen Table that otherwise would not have existed.

Well, absolutely, because we did not have a press. There was no women of color press that was doing the kind of publishing that Kitchen Table did, particularly since we were publishing all women, of whatever sexual orientation, and women of all nationalities, races, and ethnicities. One of the things that we arrived at in the early days—and we moved the press to New York in the fall of 1981. We had not really officially launched until the fall of '81, or announced that there was such a thing as Kitchen Table. We certainly had not done any publishing at that point. But we had made the decision—when we talked about who qualified as a woman of color, we came up with, after much discussion, that our definition of women of color was any woman who identified with the indigenous people of her respective nation or land. One of the reasons we put it that way is that there are people of European heritage in Argentina, for example, Jewish women. Are they Latinas or not? Well, I think we could argue that indeed they are, because of where they were born, and the language they speak, and the culture that they're a part of.   So, we made that decision that we were not looking for photographs of people. We just wanted to know if you identified with the indigenous people of your respective nation or country.

To me, that was a very sophisticated decision. And it was a very principled decision. And it's hard to explain, Keeanga, what it was like—in this historical moment—what it was like to have little or nothing. It's hard to explain how ridiculed and how debased and how much insult women of color and feminists of color and lesbians of color in particular—how much we faced in that regard. During a time when gay people can get married, and Beyoncé says she's a feminist, it's difficult to explain what we were up against in the late 1970s.

How were your politics influenced by socialist feminism? What was socialist feminism and how did they fit into the feminist movement at this time?

And there were racial divides at the socialist feminist conference. So it's not like there was ever any place where we could go and it was just perfect, or even acceptable. [laugh] Moderately acceptable. It was always like striking out into new territory. Having to make a place for ourselves and a way for ourselves. One of the things that the socialist feminists had organized were women's unions. Are you familiar with the women's unions?

No. What was the relationship between socialist feminism and the women's unions?

In the 1970s, there were women's unions—socialist feminist women's unions—all over the United States. I don't know how many there were. I think there were at least twenty or thirty of them, maybe even more. But they were women's unions that were connected to each other. That's what they called themselves.

So ours was the Boston Women's Union. And there were similar socialist feminist organizations all around the nation. I'm sure Chicago had one. I know California or Berkeley, Bay Area, had one. I can't tell you all the places they were. But that would be fertile ground for you to do some research on, too. It's fascinating to me that these are politics that you undoubtedly would identify with, and yet here's a chapter of that history that you don't know anything about. There was a network—a national network of socialist feminist women's unions. They were all aligned with each other. I don't know if they had conferences or not. They may very well have had conferences. Because I actually attended the socialist feminist conference in 1974. '74? Let me just think. '75. In 1975. The summer of 1975, there was a socialist feminist conference at Antioch College in Ohio. And it was attended by hundreds of women, if not more than hundreds. It might have been a thousand women. It was very well attended. And that's where I met Cheryl Clarke, actually. But that conference had the familiar problems around the marginalization of women of color. There were relatively few women of color there. The reason that I went is because we had met, and had begun working with socialist feminists in the Boston area by that time. Because there was a strong Boston women's union in Boston, and we met them because of them inviting us to get involved with the Committee to End Sterilization Abuse. That was my first kind of organizational interaction with the socialist feminists in the Boston area. And a couple years later, it was socialist feminists primarily who organized against the Hyde Amendment and started the Abortion Action Coalition. They were doing other things. I can't tell you all the issues that they were working on, because I was not a part of their organizational structure.

But around the issue of sterilization abuse, and abortion rights, those are two of the major initiatives that we worked with socialist feminists on. And we did so for quite some time. So we're talking about a few years. And some of the people who I knew from that era, I'm still friends with to this day. The white women in the socialist feminist movement had been a part of the left, of course. We were age peers, women in our twenties and thirties, for the most part. And they had been I'm sure involved with the movement to end the war in Vietnam, campus organizing, et cetera. These were women who actually understood that you could not really deal with sexism and the exploitation of women if you didn't look at capitalism and also at racism. So unlike some of the other feminists—cultural feminists, radical feminists, lesbian separatists, bourgeois feminists, and mainstream feminists—unlike all of those groups of feminists, socialist feminists had a race and class analysis . . . and thought that addressing race and class were important. Whether they did so expertly and without any mistakes, that of course was not true. We sometimes knocked heads around what we perceived as their racism and perhaps sometimes their classism or elitism or whatever. It's not like it was all smooth sailing, because we were organizing across identities. We were doing that intersectional organizing. But of all the feminists, of the varieties of feminists that I just described, socialist feminists were best aligned, as far as I'm concerned, with the work of Combahee. Because they had a race and class analysis that was actually a solid race and class analysis as opposed to, "Oh, I don't really care if people are different." The baloney, you know. "I don't really see color." "Well, time to go to the ophthalmologist."

The socialist feminists, the Boston Women's Union was already looking at the issue of sterilization abuse before members of Combahee started participating. We got involved and we had what was called the Committee to End Sterilization Abuse in Boston. CESA. There was a really incredibly brilliant and wonderful leader around sterilization abuse, whose name is Dr. Helen Rodríguez-Trías. When we first met her, she was Helen Rodríguez. She was a Puerto Rican woman who was a pediatrician. And she was just incredible, as far as inspiring us and teaching us about—strategically—how we could indeed bring this issue to the fore.

We would have demonstrations at Boston City Hospital. I lived in the South End at that time, where Boston City Hospital was. And that was the hospital for poor people—the public hospital in Boston. There was also a very infamous antiabortion case. Have you ever heard of Dr. Kenneth Edelin?

No.

Dr. Kenneth Edelin. He was an ob-gyn—and he was Black. He did a legal abortion in Boston City Hospital, and he was tried for manslaughter.

Oh my god, wow.

This had to have been—this is after *Roe v. Wade*. So abortion was legal, right? And the compulsory pregnancy people—they had been looking for an ideal test case. And with whoever was around during the procedure cooperating, they brought him up on charges. He went on trial. We used to go to the courthouse, where his trial happened. Fortunately, he was acquitted. We were triumphant.

So we were involved in his case. And then there was the case of Ella Ellison, a Black woman wrongfully convicted of robbery and first-degree murder, who was serving two life sentences. We were involved in the organizing to free Ella Ellison, and eventually all charges against her were dropped. We were involved in a lot of things. The Committee to End Sterilization Abuse was connected with CARASA, the Committee for Abortion Rights and Against Sterilization Abuse, in New York City.

In those days, if you were politically involved, particularly as socialist feminists and leftists, you were always studying and reading, you know? So we learned a lot about population control. The worldwide population movement. Eugenics. Probably it was during that period that I first read some biographical material about Margaret Sanger and the founding of Planned Parenthood.

We were very serious. And it was great. It's like I got my education in college and in grad school, but I got another kind of education just being in the movement. And as I said, we were successful in Boston in eventually getting legislation or regulations to ban sterilization abuse. Sterilization abuse was happening to women of color all over the country and in Puerto Rico. It was so common in Puerto Rico that they just called it "the operation." In Spanish. "*La operación*," or however you would say it.

So many women had been sterilized in Puerto Rico. Native American women were disproportionately sterilized against their will or without their consent. Black women, particularly Black women who were receiving government entitlements, were sterilized. There were two sisters—the Relf sisters in Alabama. The Relf sisters, Mary Alice, who was twelve years old and Minnie Lee, fourteen, had developmental disabilities. They were sterilized as teenagers. So it was pandemic, you know? And we were trying to deal with that.

Those are some of the things we were doing in the early days. But those contradictions—I talked a lot about the socialist feminists because we shared political ideology with them, and political priorities—the radical feminists saw patriarchy and sexism as being the primary contradiction. We did some organizing with them as well, because they were strong on violence against women. I had one friend in particular, Lisa Leghorn; she was one of the people who helped to start the first battered women's shelter in Boston, which was called Transition House.

We worked with anybody who we could work with, whoever it was viable to work with. And it was a wonderful time, because we were young, we were idealistic, we were energetic, and in the case of Black feminists in Combahee, we were making it up from scratch.

Let me ask you about that. Because you said that you began as a chapter of the National Black Feminist Organization.

That's right.

And then you became the Combahee River Collective. What led to the change, the switch?

We wrote a little bit about that in the statement itself, I believe. We were not getting the kind of support and resources we felt we needed to have as a chapter of NBFO. Because NBFO was a grass-roots organization trying to be a national organization without the kinds of infrastructure or funding that, for example, the National Organization for Women had.

NBFO, I think, in some of its aspirations and its perspectives, wanted to be like NOW. That kind of a broad, maybe electorally focused, not necessarily by any means radical or left, formation. But a major thing was that they didn't have the resources to actually service chapters. And there were chapters in Chicago and Washington. I think some out in California. There were chapters around the country, and it was very difficult for NBFO—I think the national office was in New York City—it was difficult for them to really meet the needs of a chapter organization, given their limited resources.

So there was that, and then there was also the fact that their politics were not the politics that we were developing in Combahee. Because we were very fortunate to have people in the founding group of Combahee who had extensive experience in other movements, including the Black Panthers, the peace movement to end the war in Vietnam, and in socialist organizations. There was one person in particular, Sharon Bourke—she had worked at the Institute for the Black World. And she also was a highly sophisticated, well-educated Marxist. So, we had people who had those politics. And us coming together, at a certain point, we said, "You know, NBFO is just not the right fit for us. Let's be independent." And that's what we did.

How big was your group in Boston?

It was never huge. And I have to say, over the years, I have liked being in small grassroots local groups. It's not that I've not ever done work on a national level—I have. It's just that for me, being in these smaller grassroots organizations that really make a difference in the landscape and in the political possibilities—in a particular place—that has always worked for me.

Combahee, because of the statement, had a much wider impact. But we still were a grassroots collective. We started by doing consciousness-raising. When we were still NBFO, we would have consciousness-raising groups, which was very popular at the time. We did that at the Cambridge Women's Center, which is probably the oldest—if not, the second-oldest—women's center in this country. I don't know how many women's centers there are left in the United States. They used to be everywhere. But as I said, we used to do consciousness-raising meetings at the women's center in Cambridge. And dozens of people came through for those meetings. But as far as the core group is concerned, I would say ten or less.

That's my recollection, that we were always a relatively small group. Starting in '77, we began having Black feminist retreats. That was an idea that I had. I was traveling around mostly the East Coast. But I was already speaking primarily on college and university campuses, because of my work in Black women's literature and Black women's studies. I had the opportunity to meet other Black feminists in different places. And I felt like wow, it's so frustrating that we're so separated. Wouldn't it be great if we could get together?

The first one was in South Hadley, Massachusetts, where Mount Holyoke is. We were using the home of a professor who became partners with one of my dear friends in college after I graduated. We asked if we could use their home for our first retreat, and that's exactly what we did. I think we had two retreats at their home. And they vacated the home for the weekend. We had them in New Jersey. We had them in Washington, DC. We had one, I think, on Cape Cod. We had seven in all.

Wow. And what was the purpose of the retreats?

It was really about—first of all—to get Black feminists together so we could talk about what it was we were trying to do. It was to address isolation that we faced as Black feminists. So it was to get us all together in one place. It was to have serious political discussion. It was to have cultural and social opportunities and outlets. It was everything. [laugh] It was multipurpose, three days of everything. There would be—there was food of a level you could not even imagine.

Because my sister and I, we loved to cook. Demita is one of the best cooks on the planet. So we would throw down. We would just absolutely throw down. And there were other people—we were all Black women of a certain generation. When I meet Black women who don't know how to cook, it's just like, "Really?"

Right, right, right.

How did that happen!? [laugh]

So there was the food, there were the books. If we had read something somewhere—the only technology at that point was to copy something or to xerox it or to mimeograph it or to ditto it. I mean, we would have like a literature table. A little literature table with books and articles. Bring enough so that everybody could have a copy of whatever it was.

Audre Lorde was involved. In fact, I think it was being around Audre that made me start thinking about how we needed to have a retreat because I had met her earlier. But anyway, Cheryl Clarke came. Gloria—who now is Akasha Hull, but at that time I don't think she had changed her name quite yet. She is one of the coeditors, of course, of *All the Women Are White, All the Blacks are Men, But Some of Us Are Brave*. All kinds of people, wonderful people who have made real contributions to the movements and also to our culture.

So let me ask you a somewhat related question. What you just said raises a couple of questions for me. One is, I'm wondering if you could say more about Audre Lorde, and her influence at this particular time when you met, and when she was a part of the Combahee retreats. But what more generally—how would you describe her contribution to the politics of Black feminism?

Audre was a key figure in the creation of the mobilizing of Black feminism as a political theory and practice. If you are familiar with her books, I particularly think of *Sister Outsider,* her book of essays. You will see that she was definitely making significant contributions as well as of course in her poetry, to what do we think of— what do we mean when we say we're Black feminists? What are Black feminist concerns? As I said, she played a pivotal role in the building of Black feminism in the United States. The fact that we got connected via Combahee I think was very important for all concerned, because I think for her—you know, I think this may be somewhere in writing, but I certainly know it to be true—that for her it was like finding a really important community that before that, she didn't necessarily have in the same way. Although Black feminism was building in New York City as well. So it's not that there was nothing there, but Combahee, as you know, was unique in the breadth of its politics. Audre definitely identified as a socialist as well. And she had had extensive political experience working in leftist movements prior to being involved with Combahee. So she brought that to Combahee, or to our retreats.

The retreats resulted in an ongoing network among those who participated in them, when we weren't at a retreat. All of a sudden, as a result of having our retreats, we suddenly had people, sometimes in our own geographic location, sometimes elsewhere, who we could reach out to, plan things with, do projects with, et cetera. The reason I thought of us having retreats—and it was I who thought of the idea of us doing that—as I recollect, I was at a Modern Language Association convention in Chicago. And I guess it was probably December '78—or it could have been '77. I'm not sure. I can't remember. But Audre was at that convention. I don't think I talked to her about the retreat idea, but it was just so clear to me, because I was getting to go and meet people in various places, who were Black feminists. And I just thought, we need to kind of organize this and institutionalize this. Not in the sense of being a bureaucracy, but we need to figure out a way that the experiences I was having—because they were so valuable—and the opportunities to meet other Black feminists, that we needed to do that in an organized fashion.

So that's where the idea for the retreats came from. And of course, you know, when I got back and we talked about it in Combahee, everybody thought that was a great idea. And then we went about the work of organizing them. And they were well organized. We had to communicate only by letter or by phone. We would have a literature table at our retreats, which were generally in people's homes. That is, people who had large enough homes to accommodate us. And that was generally not people who were part of the collective. Our first retreat was at the home of a professor whose name is Jean Grossholtz. She's a political scientist and emeritus at Mount Holyoke. And the first retreat that we had was in their home in South Hadley. And it was a large home. But as I said, wherever we were, whether it was in a house—you know, like wherever we were—and as I said, almost all the retreats—I don't think we ever had a retreat in a public setting—we would have a literature table. And literature in those days was xeroxes. And even mimeographed. That's what literature was for Black women who were interested in feminism or in politics that included a gender analysis. There were no books. [laugh]

As I said, they were very well organized. They generally went from Friday through Sunday. And I would imagine sometimes people arrived on Thursday so that Friday was a full day. We talked about politics. We talked about organizing. I'm sure we talked about spirituality. We would have cultural performances, usually on Saturday evening. There is a stunning example of that that occurred at a retreat that we had in New Haven. And one of the people who's still—she was on the panel at the June Jordan Symposium in 2016. Her name is Sharon Page Ritchie. Sharon was an accomplished belly dancer. And she always said that she wanted to dance for us. And so, at this particular retreat, we were able to have that occur. And when I say it was stunning, it was stunning. Because it was like we were on another plane and on another level. You know, someone who you thought you knew in a particular way, as just another good sister, turns out to be this incredibly accomplished artist in a realm that we would never even have thought.

And, of course, a lot of reading. Readings. Because there were a lot of poets involved . . . with the retreats. Audre, and Cheryl Clarke, and Akasha Gloria Hull. We talked about anything that conscious Black feminists would be talking about at that time. I think our major goal, at least as I would describe it—our major goal was how do we establish Black feminism functionally so it has actual political impact upon which way forward, for all the groups of people we cared about. I mean, if we were involved—and we were—in working on sterilization abuse and reproductive freedom, we might have been talking about that. I can't tell you. I really can't tell you. The retreats were also a time for healing and spirituality.

Why was that important?

If you're asking why it occurred, as opposed to why it was important—well, actually, the answer to both of those questions could be the same. Because we were Black women. Our value systems were not shaped primarily or initially by the airless ideological sectarianism of the white European male left. They were not. We came from a different place. We came out of Black homes, Black neighborhoods, and Black culture. Black people, as I have observed us over the decades, are always interested in cultural practices and cultural expression. That's why most of US culture that's worth anything was created by us. As Beverly, my sister says, if it wasn't for Black people, the only thing you would be able to listen to on the radio is news.

Can we talk about your objectives? What did you see ultimately as the goal of your work? Because you talk about being a relatively small organization . . .

Right.

. . . but a serious organization. Serious about political ideas and serious about political activism. What was the goal of your organizing?

I think our goal first of all was to make a political place for people like ourselves. We were marginalized in the Black movement, in the Black liberation movement, certainly in the Black nationalist movement. And we were marginalized in the white feminist movement, for different reasons. One of the reasons we were marginalized in the Black movement, besides sexism and misogyny, was also homophobia. A lot of us were indeed lesbians, and we— including myself, at this time I was coming out. Some people had been lesbians for longer. So they weren't coming out simultaneous with their involvement with Combahee. But for me, those things kind of went together.

So, as I said, we were marginalized in Black contexts. We were marginalized and not understood in white feminist or women's liberation contexts. We needed to have a place of our own. We needed to have a place where we could define our political priorities and act upon them. And that's where identity politics come from. I explain this over and over and over again. I believe that the Combahee River Collective statement is the first place that the term "identity politics" actually appears. I've asked people about this through the years—I'm not just asserting it. I ask anybody who I think might have the depth of knowledge and of reading and research and experience politically to answer that question, "Did you ever see it anywhere else before?" And the answer is always "no."

So this is one of the questions I had as a follow-up, so it actually flows from what you were just discussing. And that is about identity politics. I think that you have really clarified sort of what Combahee meant by identity politics in response to the way that the right sort of abuses the term. That if you're not of a certain race, ethnicity, or gender, then that becomes an invitation to chastise or castigate you and sort of dismiss anyone who doesn't have any of those characteristics.

But however the right wing got ahold of identity politics and began using it as their whipping boy and their whipping girl, what we meant by identity politics when we originated the terminology was wholly different. What we were saying is that we have a right as people who are not just female, who are not solely Black, who are not just lesbians, who are not just working class, or workers—that we are people who embody all of these identities, and we have a right to build and define political theory and practice based upon that reality. That was all we were trying to say. That's what we meant by identity politics. We didn't mean that if you're not the same as us, you're nothing. We were not saying that we didn't care about anybody who wasn't exactly like us. One of the things I used to say, and of course I've had so many speaking engagements I have taglines at this point [laugh] of things that I've said more than once, is that it would be really boring only to do political work with people who are exactly like me.

That's what the right pretends that we mean by identity politics, a very narrow version. And unfortunately because identity politics often have been first introduced to younger people by academics who have a partial understanding of what the depths of it would be, they are also confused about it too. Trigger warnings and safe spaces and microaggressions—those are all real, but the thing is, that's not what we were focused upon.

Mm! So I wonder if you could say more about that. And let me—I'll just add that I think that there's certainly a right-wing kind of ridiculous caricature of identity politics. But I think that the concept is also sort of seen in a particular way by liberals or the left, in that for some the notion of identity politics seems to be that unless you suffer a particular kind of oppression, that you have no role in the struggle against it. And so there's this real emphasis on experience as the main sort of—as the main kind of way that gives you the ability to fight a particular oppression. That if you don't have that experience, then you really have no role. And so it's almost as if by embracing one's identity, that you give up on any sort of hope or notion that there is such a thing as solidarity.

We never meant that. I mean, we actually worked in coalitions. I just described working in coalitions with socialist feminists. We worked in coalitions with other people, too. We certainly showed up for causes that might not be the expected ones for people who had the identities that we had. Demita [has] talked about standing up for union organizing, and for men of color who were being excluded from work sites and from construction jobs, because of racism. And I often cite that example, too, because I guess both of us will never forget the looks on the faces of the guys—who were primarily guys—who were demonstrating. And then we come, you know, and we demonstrate with them. You know, they didn't expect that to be the case. So as I said, we absolutely believed in coalition building and solidarity. It's a real misapprehension of what we meant by it. And I don't know why people skip it. I mean, to me, all the explanation that's needed is in the Combahee River Collective statement, about what it is we stand for, and who we think we should be working with. But as I have explained, the reason we used the term "identity politics" is that we were asserting at a time when Black women had no voice. At a time when Black women were being told to walk seven steps behind and have babies for the nation. At a time when Stokely Carmichael/Kwame Ture said—when asked what is the position of the Black woman in the Black struggle, and his response was that Black women's position was to be prone. He actually meant supine.

Now is a time when much solidarity is needed, because the nation-state is in free-fall. It's not like I'm a worshipper of the nation-state. That's not what I'm saying at all. But it is a little bit unsettling when you see what was thought to be basic assumptions about how that nation-state functioned go completely out the window. [laugh] This is a time for solidarity. I mean it's like just because I—and I'm doing a theoretical "I" here, or a figurative "I"—just because I have health coverage doesn't mean I shouldn't be standing in solidarity with those who stand to lose it under this regime. Just because I have a US passport and full legal status in the United States doesn't mean I'm not supposed to be standing in solidarity with people who are undocumented. Who have every right to be here as well. So, as I said, it's a misunderstanding and a distortion of what it was that we stood for. And I think that sometimes that notion that you just outlined as, "If I don't have a particular identity, I'm not allowed to work on a particular issue"—that sounds to me like an excuse. That sounds to me like Okay, so that's what somebody decides if they're not really willing to go there, and go through the struggle of crossing boundaries and working across differences. The concept of *This Bridge Called My Back* is an incredibly powerful one, and that book was catalytic in the women's movement, and in certain parts of the left. Bernice Johnson Reagon's essay, which was not originally an essay, it was an article based upon a speech—that concludes *Home Girls*—I always tell people, the reason "Coalition Politics: Turning the Century" is the last piece in the book is because that's what I wanted people to leave the book with: the idea of working together across differences.

Coalitions. "This Bridge Called My Back" as a concept. Why are those so important?

Because of the fact that that's the only way we can win. The only way that we can win—and before winning, the only way we can survive is by working with each other, and not seeing each other as enemies. There's far too much of the perspective of: "You're not like me. I'm not like you. I'm not a transgender person. I don't give a damn whether you can go to a bathroom or not. And the fact that you're being murdered summarily, and that your income levels keep you in poverty far more likely than somebody who is cisgender—that's not my problem!" Those are bad politics. Really, really bad politics. And the reason it's important, as I said, is because that's how we win, and that's how we survive in the meantime.

There are ethical principles of struggle that you can see in any significant political intervention in history. You will see—one of the things that you should see in positive movements forward toward justice—not toward power—because there are many interventions that were just about the accrual of power, where you didn't really have that mentality and that principle of "We must all be in this together." But if it's a forward movement toward justice, you will see that people of different backgrounds and different places in a social structure actually at times come together. The abolitionist movement comes to mind. Because there were white people who actually stepped away from their white skin privilege at a critical time in US history, because they could see as plain as the nose on their face that enslaving other human beings was wrong. And they decided, like, "Okay, yeah, I guess I'm white, but I guess I love humanity more." And of course, there were people who were abolitionists who were racists. Who really thought that Black people were inferior to white people. I'm not that big of a fool that I think [laugh] that everything was just . . . lovely, and everybody was just really conscious and open. No. I mean, there were abolitionists who actually thought Black people were inferior, and actually wished for them, once we were freed, to get on the first boat sailing. [laugh] "Go back somewhere else, not here!" But be that as it may, they still lost social standing, paid prices, speaking out for people whose situation they didn't have to be concerned about—what difference did it make to them? You know, they were still white in the United States. Things could have been really nice, you know?

That's a great example of when people see an incredible wrong, an incredible injustice, and they decide that justice is more important than their status and their privilege. And those are models that we need to adhere to, I believe. I love when we see examples of people pushing themselves far beyond the status quo and far beyond the average, and speaking up and speaking out and acting for justice. I always say that the people I can work with are the people with whom I share political values and goals and priorities. So that means just about anybody as far as ethnicity, race, gender, national origin, sexual orientation, gender identity. Et cetera, et cetera, et cetera. I don't have a litmus test for, like, "I only work with certain kinds of people who share my specific identities." I'm going to be a political idiot if I only work with Black lesbian feminists and refuse to work with anybody else. I mean, I wouldn't know the things that I know *about Black feminism* and about organizing if the only people I had ever worked with were Black feminists who were lesbians. Don't get me wrong. I have learned a tremendous amount from working with people whose specific identities I share, but I also would have lost a lot if I had never worked with people who are different from myself.

So let me ask you, as the sort of last thing, what is the state of Black feminism today? Because we were talking earlier, and there seems to be somewhat of a revival, at least in the interest of Black feminism. I think that was clear from the Socialism 2017 conference, where on both occasions that you and Demita spoke, there were literally hundreds of people who came to hear it and see what you all had to say. And so, why do you think that is?

I don't know. I really don't know, Keeanga . . . [about] explicitly Black feminist organizing at this time. I don't know what Black feminists are doing. I know of some organizations like Black Women's Blueprint. I have spent more time with younger people involved in Black Lives Matter organizing in recent years than I have with Black women involved in specifically feminist organizing. I think that Black feminism is strong, because we have built some understandings and also some organizations and organizing projects that address some of the issues that we thought were critical to address, like violence against women. There is available a nuanced Black women's perspective on how you address violence against women. Not everybody partakes of it, of course. But there are real manifestations that the work that we did and the priorities that we had have indeed been expanded upon and put forward and maintained.

But as I said, I can't tell you much about the state of Black feminism at the present time. And I'm not even clear that there's a Black feminist resurgence. I'm not sure of the evidence for that, except for some people in popular culture having recently gotten good responses to them asserting that this is something that people should pay attention to and even be supportive of. I don't really—I don't know. I'd love to know what you see in that regard. And I also don't think that the response at the socialism conference is one that would necessarily be applicable across the board. Because I think that that was an audience—I'm not dismissing the incredible outpouring, because I know people had choices about where they were during the times of those presentations. But I think that the people who attended that conference were people who were kind of like the prime partakers of Black feminist theory and practice, because of where they were coming from politically. And I think also that the words of Combahee and your work, too, that was recognizable to them. It was familiar. And then there were people there who did know about Combahee and they wanted to check it out. It was a perfect context. Perfect context.

Well, I do think that there has been—I wouldn't say necessarily a revival in organization, per se. But I do think that there definitely has been a resurgence in interest in the politics of Black feminism and what that means. And I think it expresses itself in different ways. I think the fact that Beyoncé in particular identified herself as a feminist raised questions about what that means and what that is,

**to a much broader audience. I think that . . . the strug-
gle around trans women of color has raised the politics
of Black feminism, which has been a kind of framing that
trans activists have applied to . . .**

Yes, which is wonderful, isn't it?

**to a much broader audience. I think the fact that the two
sort of leading organizations of the Black Lives Matter
movement—Black Lives Matter, hashtag Black Lives Matter, and the Black Youth Project, who consciously sort of
evoke the politics and ideas of Black feminism . . . in whatever way that means to them, has certainly led to a curiosity and interest in what those politics are. And so those
are all relatively new phenomena. I think even in 2011,
the emergence of SlutWalk demonstrations, and the idea
that we have to struggle against rape culture, and that
women have the right to present themselves in whatever
way that they please . . . a combination of these things has
led at least to a questioning of or a curiosity about what
is Black feminism, and why are all these other organizers
and people who are involved in politics always talking
about Black feminism? And maybe this is something that
I should investigate further.**

Right, right. And you've given some good examples. Particularly
Black Lives Matter. When I said that I know more about what is
going on with Black Lives Matter organizing than I do about Black
feminist organizing, you in some ways have corrected me and
reminded me that, wait a minute, major organizations doing Black
Lives Matter organizing around the criminal violence of the police
consider themselves to be doing so from a Black feminist perspec-

tive. So yes, that's a major example. And the other ones that you gave as well. And I think having the book come out in this context—great idea, great timing. The fortieth anniversary of Combahee seems to coincide with an upsurge of concern and interest about the politics of Black feminism. I tried to figure out terms of how to talk about the Black feminism of Combahee and Black feminism in other contexts. And I came up with a good way to say it, in an email a few weeks ago. Because I was trying not to be dismissive of other types of Black feminism. I might not have called what we did "original" Black feminism, but instead wrote that the reason Combahee's Black feminism is so powerful is because it's anticapitalist. One would expect Black feminism to be antiracist and opposed to sexism. Anticapitalism is what gives it the sharpness, the edge, the thoroughness, the revolutionary potential.

BEVERLY SMITH

KEEANGA-YAMAHTTA TAYLOR: I'm wondering if you could tell me when you became a feminist or identified as a feminist, and what were some of the factors in your background that kind of led you down that particular political orientation.

BEVERLY SMITH: I would say one of the most important experiences I have is that Barbara and I—and you may well know this—grew up in a family, in a household, specifically, that was all women.

Oh, yes. I didn't hear her phrase it quite that sharply, but that's an important thing to be aware of.

Yes. And I think—well, there are lots of reasons why I feel that that was an important part of my orienting toward feminism. And one of those things I would say about it is because everything that needed to be done in our household was done by women.

When my family moved to the house where we spent most of our years, it was a two-family house. And when we moved there, our aunt, our mother's sister, lived upstairs with her husband. So there was a period of like I would say three or four years when there was a man in the household—my aunt's husband . . . even when he was there, I don't remember anyone sort of like—not only not deferring to him, but I don't remember anyone saying like, "Oh well, we had to get Bill because only he can do this," and whatever. I don't remember that kind of behavior, although he did exercise authority. But after he left, it really was an all-female household. And so, as I said—everything that needed to get done, women were doing it.

And what kind of work outside of the home were the women in your house doing?

Our mother worked as a supermarket clerk, as like an assistant manager perhaps. I'm not sure exactly what that title was.

Barbara may have told you that she had a bachelor's in education, and that she was trained as a teacher. But unfortunately she was never really able to practice her profession. There were several reasons. One reason was because she had the necessity of earning a living as soon as possible, because she was supporting us, of course, and her mother, who could not really have worked outside of the home because she was taking care of us.

Right.

So that was the division of labor. And then our aunt worked as a clerk, or administrative assistant, but her title was clerk, at the Cleveland Public Library. It was the main library, and the Cleveland system was huge.

My aunt worked in a special division that was based upon the personal library of one of the founders of the Cleveland Public Library, and he had certain interests, like he was interested in folklore, religion. He was interested in Asia, which was called "Orientalia" at that point. There were a lot of Korans [laugh]. There was an exhibit hall, like a foyer or something, all before you went into the library part, with the books. And there were Korans there, and other things.

So those were the two women who worked outside of the house. But when we were first born and were living in our first home, we had a great aunt, in fact, our great aunt Phoebe, who we call[ed] Auntie, who was the first person to come up from the South to Cleveland. I'm not exactly sure when that would have been. Probably sometime in the '20s. She was a terrific cook, and that's how she earned her living. When we were born, she was still working—I'm pretty sure that she was working for this millionaire at that time, in his house. She would stay out there during the week and then she would come home probably on the weekends or her days off.

How do you think the experiences of the women in your household impacted your own sort of consciousness or ideas about the world?

One thing I would say—in describing the job that my aunt who worked at the library had, and then I'm thinking of my great aunt, who worked at this private girls' school, even though neither of them had the whatever it would have required—probably white skin and being male—to actually put forth and work with all of their gifts, both of them had incredible talent.

Not so much academic, necessarily, although my aunt was really great academically. She was second in her class in high school. And my great aunt, I used to refer to this particular [great] aunt as my first Black studies teacher, because she would like tell us incredible things. I knew about Marian Anderson and, you know, the Daughters of the American Revolution, and then her singing at the Lincoln Memorial. I heard that growing up. She would talk about that often. She would talk about Eleanor Roosevelt.

I remember once she talked about the play *The Merchant of Venice*. She was talking about how Portia, in *The Merchant of Venice*—she's a woman who is, I think, defending her father, the merchant. And she's a woman. So Shakespeare wrote this story where a woman acted as a lawyer. And of course we know how long ago that was. Our great aunt, who I've been telling you about, took particular note of it.

So what I would say [is] they were very gifted. And also, they all had whatever it took in order to pursue their interests and their gifts and develop their talent. Another great aunt who I would like to tell you about, because I think it's relevant, was a certified or qualified teacher down south. When she came up to Cleveland, of course she didn't have any certification. I'm not even sure whether she would have been of age to pursue teaching up in Cleveland anyway. So what she did was—I tell people that if she had been white, she would have been considered a nanny. But [laugh] because she was Black, no one would ever have referred to her as that, that way.

She took care of lots of very well-off children, and she was a teacher. I mean, she taught us amazing things. She was so creative, and we were always doing like little craft projects and things like that. And at a certain point, because money was always an issue for her, as it was for all of the family, she decided that she was going to become a practical nurse.

There was a school in Cleveland, a public school, although they may have sent [her] to the adult education. There may have been tuition involved. She lied about her age in order to get into the program, because she was too old as far as the requirements were at that time. And she did very, very well. But then unfortunately—she had arthritis, and she had an accident and fell, and she was not able to continue, because she became disabled as a result of the arthritis and the fall.

I'm assuming that you all talked about politics and the news, and what was happening in the world.

All the time. I remember when——I guess it was when the lunch counter sit-ins were happening, I remember my grandmother saying, "They say we're not supposed to trade at Woolworth's." The reason she used that phrase was that was an old-fashioned way of talking, if you were living and growing up in rural Georgia. You went into town to trade. And so she said, "I hear we're not supposed to trade at Woolworth's."

She was very, very active in the community, too. She worked at the polls. She was in every kind of club you can imagine, in relationship to the church. She did huge amounts of volunteer work that no one would really recognize as such. Every fund drive they had——people used to go door to door to collect for things like the Cancer Society, you know, or the March of Dimes, things like that. She was always doing that, and we would go with her.

So, yeah, there was a great interest in what was going on in the world. There was a great habit of discussing politics. The grownups would be downstairs——in our first place, we had up- and downstairs. And I realized that it seemed like the grown-ups were always talking about race. I might not have put it in those terms, but I remember wondering, when I was very young, "I wonder why grown-ups always talk about race."

I didn't see it necessarily as something that Black grown-ups did. To me it was just——"Well, I guess that's just what they do. That's just what grown-ups talk about."

You two must have been coming of age politically perhaps actively during the civil rights movement.

Oh, absolutely. I remember——like the remark that I told you, that my grandmother made about boycotting Woolworth's, I remember that. I remember hearing about the Supreme Court decision. I was aware of that, even though that was 1954, and we were born in '46, so we were seven during that time period.

We also, a couple years earlier, were aware of the presidential campaign, when Eisenhower was running for the first time, because he had a slogan. His nickname was "Ike," I-K-E. And so he had a slogan, "I like Ike." We heard that, and we would repeat it, and one of our great aunts, the one who was the cook, used to laugh and thought it was so funny that, you know, we were aware of this slogan.

Little Rock—[we were] very aware of Little Rock and when they integrated Central High School, because that was during the Eisenhower administration, the second administration. And that was really, I think, the first nationally noticed skirmish, more than a skirmish—battle—in the civil rights movement. We were aware of the bus boycott, the Montgomery bus boycott. I remember—pretty much anything and everything that happened [laugh] in the civil rights movement, we were aware of it, because we'd be watching it on television.

I remember particularly, I think this was when we were in junior high, New Orleans was integrating the schools. And they were really hateful. One of the things I remember from that time is that there were white mothers—some of them with their hair in curlers. And I remember these white mothers screaming at the Black children, just like being so horrible to the Black children. And I was so young, I remember thinking, how could these women, how could they be mothers? Because it did not accord with my concept of what a mother was like.

But in terms of the questions you're asking, I knew that was going on.

When did you become politically active?

I would say we became politically active—well definitely in high school. I can't remember exactly. I would say probably sixteen, seventeen.

What were you doing? What was the source of your activity?

One of the things, I don't know exactly how we hooked up with this, but we actually were quite involved with CORE. The Congress on—what is it—the Congress [on] Racial Equality?

Yes.

CORE was an organization that initiated the Freedom Rides. But in Cleveland, the big issue was de facto segregation. And CORE was very involved in that. I've told people this recently—one of the things we used to do when we were in high school was a lot of picketing of the board of education, which was downtown, because of the issue of de facto segregation.

And specifically the issue was that the school system kept choosing to build schools in all-white neighborhoods and areas, which prevented the possibility of integrated schools, because of where they placed the schools. This was a big, big issue. And in fact, there was a minister, a white minister, who lay down in front of a bulldozer on one of these school sites, and the bulldozer operator didn't know he was there, and he was killed.

Wow.

Yeah. Yeah, it was pretty darn intense. So we were involved with CORE. We would go down and picket at the school board. And then we would go back to our high school and be honor students.

We met Fannie Lou Hamer—it probably had something to do with CORE. She had probably come and spoken somewhere, and then we went back to someone's house and had a party, in the basement. I remember Fannie Lou Hamer, sitting in this chair, and Barbara and I were sitting on the floor, at her feet. I remember that so distinctly. I remember what she looked like. I remember her hair. And one thing I want to say is that I think it was so amazing about our experience in the civil rights movement, and specifically with CORE, is that these were some extremely and supportive and respectful and concerned adults.

The head of CORE in Cleveland at that time was a woman. And I think that may well have had a lot to do with why we were welcomed, and why—the spirit or the values and processes of the organization [were] comfortable enough for us very young people to be involved with the organization.

Also, my sister and I were very involved in the school boycott. And we boycotted. We stayed out of school. They had set up Freedom Schools all over the city on the day of the boycott. My sister and I would go to one that was near us. It was at a church very near to us. So we walked over to the church. And we went in, and it was bedlam. Barbara and I read them the riot act. We said, "No, this is not what this is supposed to be." And then we started talking to them about civil rights. The civil rights movement, and what this meant.

You organized them.

"You're not supposed to be running around [laugh] like little idiots, This is serious! This is important!" [laugh] And so, I'm sure they were happy when we left! [laugh]

[laugh]

Anyway, that's just an example. We wanted to go to the March on Washington. But our aunt would not permit us to go. And one of our friends at high school who we were in class [with], she went. And we were saying, "Well, Carlotta is going."

And that didn't cut a lot of ice with our aunt. Basically she said, "You're too young." And when I think back on it, from her point of view, and from the point of view in general of the parent, I would probably come down on that side. Because she also did not know well the people that we knew and were working with from CORE. But we were so disappointed, because we really, really wanted to go.

Did you watch the coverage on television?

Oh, absolutely! Oh, yes! Absolutely. I'm one of the few people [laugh] who actually heard the speech as it was being given.

Ah! Really!

Oh yeah, absolutely. That's how we got a lot of information about the whole civil rights movement. We had magazines and newspapers and stuff. We got *Ebony* and *Jet* and the daily newspapers. But TV was a great source of information.

I remember when we *got* our first TV. Because we're old enough that when we were born, no one had TVs! It just wasn't a thing. They weren't there. But then we got a TV and we—of course as kids, we just loved it. We used to listen to the radio when we were younger, and they had programs on for kids. But we'd listen to the news, too. Let me put it another way. We heard the news.

This is a varied sort of rich set of experiences. So what happens when you both graduate from high school, and then go to college? And so how does this impact you when you leave Cleveland, when you go to college?

This is where you had a huge divergence in this experience of Barbara and me, because we went to two different schools. They were different in the sense that we went to two schools, but they were very different schools from each other, too. I went to the University of Chicago, and Barbara went to Mount Holyoke.

Mm. [laugh] Very different.

Yeah. So Barbara goes to Mount Holyoke, smallish school, college, not your university. 1,600 students, I think, total. Barbara was involved in activism pretty much from the moment she got there.

And in fact, if I'm not mistaken, probably the first activism she was involved in was trying to get the rules, the restrictive rules that they had for the girls, lifted, because I think they had something called parietal hours. I don't even think it was an issue about how late they could stay out, because they were in the woods. [laugh] We used to call it "Mount Holyoke of the Woods." [laugh]

The issue was, like, the circumstances under which men could actually come into the dormitories.

And I think they called those parietal hours. Men could only come into the dormitories only one day a week, on a weekend. I think it was Sundays—probably Sunday.

But the thing is, men could not come to rooms. They had these little parlors down I think on the first floor of the dorms, where you could have a gentleman caller or whatever come in. A boy. [laugh] Specifically. Because we were "girls" and "boys."

That was some of the first organizing I think my sister did. Also,

I think anti–Vietnam War activity during her first year. In fact, I think when she came out to visit me—I'm trying to think whether it was my first year—yeah, it was my first year, Barbara was able to come and visit me in Chicago. I remember she and I went to an antiwar demonstration. This would have been in early—sometime in '66, I think.

We went to this demonstration. And there was this slightly older white guy. He may even have still been a college student, but a bit older. So he was talking to us and found out that we were in college. And then had the nerve to turn on us and say, "Well, you're just—you're bourgeois." You know, "You're just . . . " I mean, this white guy? [laugh] We're at the demonstration.

I do remember that I felt attacked by this guy, because we came from the wrong background. That was not the first time that people made some assumptions about where we came from, in terms of our background.

But what happened for me—the first year I was there, our class at Chicago, entering class of I think maybe around seven hundred or so, and we had about I think twenty-three Black students. And that was four times more than they had ever had in any entering college class.

When you got to University of Chicago . . .

So what was the political scene?

Yeah. Did you get involved?

My first year, I told you about how we had a small number of Black students. There were some other Black students—well, at least one guy who was a graduate student who I met. And so we formed a little group where we would get together.

And it wasn't like heavy political or anything. It was more like a support group. But we also knew that being a Black student there definitely had political implications. We were dealing with racism pretty much from the day we got there, in terms of things that professors said.

We had a lot of what they call[ed] general education courses at Chicago. But there was a course I didn't take, which was one of the social science courses. It was history and who knows what else. But what were they studying? They were studying the history of slavery. A lot of the other Black girls were taking this class.

And I remember them one day coming back from the lecture, because you know, we would have our individual sections and we would have the big lecture. They came back from the lecture. They were distraught. Why? Because the professor who had given the lecture was talking about Black women slaves and rape. And he said, "You can't rape a Black woman, because a Black woman is always ready."

What?!

Yeah, they were distraught. Distraught. I don't know whether any of them were crying, but there were a whole bunch of them. Oh yeah, there was much crap. Much crap.

The second year there was a young woman I had met in Cleveland through my civil rights activism. And I don't know exactly how I met her, but I definitely remember being at meetings with her and her being involved in the school boycott. I knew her before that time. I was always very intimidated by her, because she was so—she was very like, "I'm right. I have the [word from] on high." She had kind of a severe manner. And even though these terms weren't used at that point, I think, I realized, well, you know, she's politically correct and I'm not. And basically what happened is that she sort of turned what I described before as a primarily Black support group, a place to get together—sure we talked about politics. I mean, what Black student would not be talking about politics in 1965, '66? Come on!

But the thing is, she gets there and she goes right to the Black nationalism, Black separatism thing. That's what became "correct." And I had the nerve—let me just put it this way. One of the few boyfriends or girlfriends I've ever had in my life, it just so happened that this guy who I had sort of a yearlong relationship with—was white. I became persona non grata. I didn't do politics in college. That shut me right down.

And so how did you get back to activism then?

Well, one thing that was interesting and unusual, I think, is that there was a woman at Mount Holyoke—Barbara and she were in the same class, so they were there for two years. And then this woman, Janet, decides to transfer, of all places, to University of Chicago. [laugh] We weren't really friends, but we did connect. And one time, in our third year, Janet invited me to go to a women's liberation meeting.

Out in the city, on the North Side. Probably never even been on the North Side. So we went to this women's lib meeting, a women's liberation meeting. And I'm there. I'm the only Black child there. Probably Janet and I were a bit younger than the other women who were there, because we were still college students.

And I'm sitting there and I'm like, "So what language are these people talking?" [laugh] I did not get it. But you know what? I was willing to go. And I remember that very vividly. And I think I might even have said, "You know, this is just very hard for me to grasp because all the stuff I've dealt with has been racial, and racist." I probably did say that a couple times. I mean I just couldn't comprehend it.

But there were some people on the faculty, a man in fact is who I'm thinking of, a historian, who was a pro-feminist, very radical, on the left. I started taking a course with him, and then I dropped it, because I just had too much work and I could drop the course and still have the correct number of courses.

But I was in there for a while, and I got a sense of what he was doing, and he was very interested in the history of the underclass, the unseen, and that included women. And that was probably my third year. My fourth year, my last quarter at college, I had a history teacher, American history, who was very progressive. And he's the only professor who ever gave me an "A" in my major.

We had to write these papers, fairly long research papers, outside of a class. And so, he was my advisor, and I decided that I would write about the relationship between the abolitionist movement and the women's movement, pretty much post—after the Civil War.

Although there was stuff that I covered undoubtedly that had to do with before the war, because, of course, there were a lot of women who were involved in the abolitionist movement throughout the century. And at the same time they had been doing women's organizing. Seneca Falls—I can't remember exactly when that was. But the thing is, I knew there was a connection. And so I wrote a paper that had to do with how these white women dealt with the fact that Black men were getting the franchise.

Mm! Mm-hmm.

And one of my regrets, not huge, but one of my regrets is I don't still have that paper. Because shortly after I finished college, I showed it to someone I worked with who was interested, and I never got it back. But that's what it was about. I know some of the sources that I used, because one of the main sources was a woman who became quite prominent in writing women's history, American women's history. So there was that.

And I never stopped paying attention to stuff, even though I wasn't an activist, because I was so politically incorrect. Stokely [Carmichael] came [laugh] to campus. I went to see Stokely my first quarter. Martin Luther King came to campus. I went to that.

I was keeping up. I knew what was happening. And in Cleveland, after my first year, when we came home after our first year of college, it just so happened [laugh] very serendipitously that Cleveland had this big riot.

So there's no way you could avoid [laugh] what was going on. It was just there. See, if I had been at a place where my politics were acceptable, I would have been doing political work. I didn't give up political work because I didn't want to be an activist. I gave it up because I didn't have anybody to do it with.

And, [laugh] you know, the beliefs that I had—for example, these people were so [laugh] what's the word? I want to say *solipsistic*. I don't know whether that's the correct word. But the thing is, they were so [laugh] inward-looking and inward-dwelling that they had no use for SDS or people who were demonstrating or working against the war.

Because, after all, you know, SDS is a white organization. Well, guess what? SDS might have been white. Most of the demonstrators at a certain point might have been white, who were demonstrating against the war. But the army, the armed forces, was very colored. And, surprise, surprise, so were the Vietnamese.

They were not white people! But I think you get a sense of what the received wisdom was.

Given your college experiences, how then did you become active in the women's liberation movement?

Well, you probably [laugh] maybe read about it, that they used to refer to people who were feminists and for women's liberation, they used to call them "women's libbers."

It was a derogatory term. And one of the things they used to refer to feminists as at that time also was "bra burners." From what I know, women never burned their bras. What happened is that at the Miss America pageant, I'm not sure what year it was, they had something called a "freedom trash can," where they threw things like bras and who knows what else, corsets and girdles, right, many, many other things, into the can. But nothing ever got burned.

I saw that, as it was happening. I watched it on television! [laugh] You know, no matter what—do you know who the Last Poets are? Are you familiar with that?

Yeah, yeah. Yes.

You know, "The revolution will not be televised"?

Mm-hmm.

Well, part of the revolution [laugh] was televised! I remember seeing that pageant and I took it all in. Took it all in. Not that I became an instant feminist. I feel like, in a way, I would call Barbara and me proto-feminists.

I'll give you an example from high school, which I think you would appreciate. The reason I majored in history is because we had a superb history teacher in high school. Extraordinary. I have decided, I tell people, the best professor I ever had was in high school. By far he was one of the most influential people in my life. Why? Because he turned me on to history.

Of course, like kids who want to go to college, then we were just all up into, oh, "Where are we going to go to college? I hope we get in." You know, applying and talking about different colleges. And our teacher, his name was Mr. Carroll, shared an office with other social studies teachers. So, once we were in there talking with Mr. Carroll—just like social time. There was another social studies teacher in there, and he could hear our conversation. So he pipes up. I think we had had him for a class. And if my exposure had only been to him, [laugh] I probably would have majored in, I don't know, zoology, economics. [laugh] He was not inspiring.

But so he pipes up, and he says, "Oh, why are you all so worried about it? You're just gonna get married." I don't remember what we said, but our teacher, Mr. Carroll—when he got a chance [to] talk with us, he said, "You all should have seen your faces, when that man said that!" He was just laughing. Because he said, "You were [laugh] ready to kill this guy!" He could see how angry we were, and how upset we were, that this man had said this. Because we were some of the best students at the school, period. Period. And there were thousands of students [laugh] at the school. The point I wanted to make though is that, I just wanted to tell you about that reaction, because that was in high school, and clearly, our instincts were just dead on. Like, "What are you talking about?" [laugh] You know? Of course, we didn't have the vocabulary. We didn't have the analysis. We didn't have any of that. But our instincts were right there.

And I think, in our particular cases, because I don't believe this uniformly—I've heard some people say that Black women in some ways are feminists by definition because of the fact that we have often had leadership roles in our communities. We have been working women—women who worked, ever since we got here. We were brought here to work.

I'm not telling you anything you don't know, but sometimes I've heard Black women characterized—"Well, you know, Black women just, you know, almost in a way definitionally are kind of feminist." Because we did some of the things that constituted liberation before other folks, mainly or namely white women. I don't believe that, but I do think in our case, because of the factors that I talked with you about, that there was what they call a substrate. There was like this foundation that nurtured us toward feminism in some ways.

We had a women's day at our church every year. Now, I don't know, I think that may well have been very common. However, I don't know whether they were doing that in white churches. I'm not sure. I would love to know. Because I have a suspicion that possibly this tradition of women's day might have been more a Black church thing.

I feel like knowing what I do as a Black person about the Black community, there are some ways in which our communities of struggle and oppression by definition have always been more open to women exerting some kind of power, if they could, more so than white women—some white women, let me not misspeak. But some white women who had privilege were more locked into "The man is doing all and I just will stay home" and whatever. I'm not saying they were happy, either, but I feel like, in our particular case, we had experiences, and lots of them, that nurtured feminism or that directed us toward [it].

For example, I had mentioned the person who was the head of the CORE chapter in Cleveland. She was a woman, and she was a serious, serious activist. She was a "player" in the sense that [laugh] when you were talking about civil rights activism in Cleveland, she would be considered by the establishment, and I think also by people in the movement, as a serious, genuine, not-to-be-toyed-with leader.

And that experience was fortunate. Fannie Lou Hamer—we met her early. So the civil rights movement itself is an example of where women's leadership can come to the fore. I remember so vividly when the Mississippi Freedom Democratic Party went to the Democratic Convention in 1964. We watched every minute, probably.

When JFK ran in 1960, that was the first time we got interested in a detailed way looking at that aspect of politics. Part of it was because we were encouraged to do that in one of our classes at school. Also it was an extremely exciting campaign. I'd say there were probably people of a lot of different ages who were drawn to that campaign in ways that I haven't quite seen anything similar since.

A lot was the symbolism. It wasn't so much that he was so extraordinary, necessarily. But eight long years of Eisenhower during the time of tremendous conservatism and quietism, and then comes along someone who is so much younger, so dynamic, with charisma.

So that was when we first started following and paying attention to those kinds of politics. I remember watching the vote when [Kennedy] was nominated. I remember who pushed him over. It was Wyoming, if I'm not mistaken. [laugh] I remember following the primaries—West Virginia was like a revelation. It was amazing.

And so then in '64, we were home from college. We watched with great attention what happened at that '64 convention. And Fannie Lou Hamer—she was there. Oh, and she was the leader, in terms of that delegation.

And that really also was a turning point in the civil rights movement. That's really what sowed the seeds for separatism, because the Democratic Party really messed up and really betrayed people who thought that they would be able to accomplish something.

Tell me about how you became involved in the Combahee River Collective.

When I saw this question, Keeanga, I thought, "Oh, well because of Barbara. End of story." And then I started thinking about it and said, "No, wait a minute. It's more complicated than that." In the fall of 1973, I was living in New York City, and I was married. We were in New York City because he had gotten a job there.

He was specifically in TV. He was a producer and director. Because of his contacts in media, he knew someone who knew someone, or you know, had some contact with *Ms.* magazine. And so through this person, I found out there was an opening at *Ms.* I worked there in the fall [of 1973], and when I was there, very soon after I came there, I met a Black woman named Margaret Sloan. And she, if I'm not mistaken, was one of the key people who founded the National Black Feminist Organization (NBFO).

And she told me that they were going to be having their first conference in New York City in, I think it was November. And of course I was very excited about that. And so, I let my sister know. And so, of course she wanted to come. And there [were] a lot of interesting people there. Before I forget, I'll just tell you, Alice Walker was there.

Barbara already knew Alice and had a relationship with Alice. So I met Alice, so that was great. Another person of that type who was very well known and probably became even more so is a woman named Faith Ringgold. I don't know if you know her name or not. But she's a terrific artist. She was one of the most probably well-thought-of and well-known Black women artists at that time.

Absolutely. I know who she is and I know her work very well.

So Faith was there. That was very exciting. She was one of the people who really stood out for me. And I met a number of other women there.

But the other thing I want to tell you about is that even before I went to *Ms.* and even before I got involved with the NBFO, I had been trying to find some kind of feminist connection in New York City. And this was really early in the women's movement, as far as I was concerned, because it was not—it wasn't like there were a thousand things around. But I found out where there were NOW meetings.

And I used to go, not a huge number of times, but I went to several NOW meetings, which met on the Upper East Side of New York. I can't remember exactly where it was, but it was some of kind of public space, like an auditorium or a hall. So I went to several NOW meetings, because that was pretty much all I could find.

Another thing that was helpful is that—I'm trying to remember her name. I think her name was Ellen Willis and I think she wrote—I'm trying to think of someone who wrote for the *Village Voice*. I think it was Ellen Willis, and she wrote a lot about the women's movement in the *Voice* during that period.

And so anyway, the reason I mentioned the *Voice* is because one of the columns, I remember, specifically in the *Voice*, was that [Willis] had a column about doctors who were women in New York City. And in fact I found my primary care doctor from that list, and also my gynecologist. So you could see that I was interested in—more than interested in finding those connections.

The reason I wanted to mention that is to indicate that I was pursuing feminism before I went to this particular conference. And so, we went to the conference. It was wonderful. In fact, this morning I was thinking—I remember writing some things about it. I had huge long subway rides to get to and from, and it was over a weekend.

And the thing is, I remember writing something about it, and I was trying to figure out whether I still had that journal. And logically, although I don't remember seeing it anytime lately, [laugh] I'm thinking, "Okay, if I remember correctly, I really should have that particular journal."

Do you remember any of the details from the NOW meetings?

Yes. In fact there's one NOW meeting I remember in particular. And one thing I'm sure you would be interested in—I was usually one of very few Black women there. The crowd was as one might expect—quite middle-class, quite white.

Right.

But one meeting I went to I never will forget, because there was a woman there named Barbara Seaman. And I'm pretty sure I might have read things by her already, but because it was New York, and because New York was one of the centers of feminists and the development of the movement, there were a lot of people who were either well known at the time or became well known. Barbara Seaman became or was one of those people, because her focus was on women's health.

So anyway, at the meeting, she had requested that she have some time to just speak to the group, and she did. And what she said was something along the lines of, "I want to share with you something that I have been noticing recently, and that I'm quite concerned about." And what she told us about was people who she knew, and people like herself, that is to say white middle-class, upper middle-class, who had experienced violence, usually from their husbands.

Because most of the women—I think if they were involved

with men, they were probably married, because of the age group. They weren't that much older than I. But the point I wanted to make is that she told one story that I remember very vividly. There was a woman who was involved in the women's movement. And she and her husband had a joint checking account, and then maybe they both had separate checking accounts as well.

And so what happened is that she had made a contribution to a women's group, and for whatever reason, she used the joint account rather than her own account, maybe because she had run out of checks. You know, just something very simple. And so because of that, her husband saw the check that she had written, and he got so angry that he threw hot coffee on her.

Yeah. That's how angry he was. And that was difficult enough. But in addition, what made it very significant was the fact that I had been hearing about these kinds of things recently and [Barbara Seaman] was asking the audience there, "Have any of you heard anything like that?" Now I don't remember the response, but that's the first time I heard anyone talk about violence against women.

Wow.

And it made such an impression on me. Well, first of all, the story itself was horrifying. I mean, like hot coffee? Are you kidding?

And it wasn't like this was a total shock. I'm sure he must have known—I'm virtually sure he would have known that she was involved in women's activities, but there was just something that set him off about the fact that it was their joint account, or maybe the fact that he saw specifically the amount of the check, because it was their joint account. Who knows?

And then, as I said, what made it even more significant was that Barbara said, "And I've heard [of] more than one incident of this sort." And at that time, there was very little going on in this country that had to do with violence against women. I suspect at that time there—yeah, this is '73. So you know, I suspect there were absolutely no shelters for women.

And so did you go to NOW meetings on a regular basis?

I didn't go to a huge number because they weren't that appealing to me, because of some of the reasons I said. You know, the women were somewhat older, although I'm not sure how much that affected me. But the fact that the group was predominantly white was not appealing to me.

And I think I also had enough sense at that time or enough understanding at that time to realize that NOW did not have the type of politics I was interested in. But it was the only thing I could find.

You began by talking about the National Black Feminist Organization conference.

It was just—it was revelatory. And one of the reasons it was amazing is that I had never heard the experiences of Black women talked about in a politically analytical way before that time.

I had also never [seen] so many Black women in one place. There were, I would say, two hundred people there, three hundred people there. I was so thrilled to think that there might be a place where I could return to doing political work.

And that's one of important things that I got from being at that conference. I thought, "Oh, so there's a way for me to be political without having my head hammered down," as I was when I was at college, because my politics are not identical with whoever else is practicing them. So that was one thing that was really compelling.

It was just so amazing to hear other Black women talk about

experiences they had that related to them being both Black and female. After that conference, one of the things that happened is that those of us who were in New York who were either at the conference themselves or maybe through the organizers of the conference, we got information about who else was there from New York City. And so, subsequent to that, I did have some contact with people who I had met there.

In one instance, through one of the women who I met there— she worked in healthcare—I was able to get a job in the New York City Health and Hospitals Corporation. That's what it was called at that time. I had just decided like a few months before, the summer of '73, that I wanted to go to public health school. So I was directing my activities towards that.

Meeting this woman and then with her help getting a job—it was on a research project at the Health and Hospitals Corporation, that was very helpful. And there were some other ones, too. I'm pretty sure we probably had at least one meeting of folks who had attended the conference.

So were there chapters formed out of the conference?

I know one of the things [Barbara] did was to contact the organizers of the conference to get names of women who lived in the Boston area. She really began organizing from that basis, in Boston. But yeah, there were definitely chapters that formed. I think there might have been one in Detroit. In terms of whether all the chapters came out of the conference, I couldn't tell you that. But there were chapters in various cities. And again, my sister knows about that. She and I think Demita [Frazier] might have gone to a conference that I think might have been in Detroit. This might have been a year later or so.

And I think it may be referred to in the Combahee River Collective statement, because I think there's something in the statement that says something like our group, that is, the Combahee River Collective, had decided to become independent of the National Black Feminist Organization, because our politics differed. Part of that process was that Barbara and I think Demita, too, may have gone to that conference, that I believe was in Detroit.

And so what were your ideas about Combahee, and how did you get involved in Boston?

I separated from my husband at the beginning of '74, and also had applied to public health school. And I went to public health school in the fall of '74. So I was in school for two years.

Because of the requirements of my program, I had to do something called a field placement. So I came to Boston and found a place—when Barbara was living in Boston at that time—and found a placement with an agency. And what they did was to provide family planning services and reproductive health services, I guess one would say, at health centers and maybe some other sites around Boston. It was a really big program, because they had a lot of health centers that were involved. And I worked for that program for about six months or so. I came out to Boston in May of '75 and then I went back to Yale in the beginning of '76 to finish my degree. Now, during the time period that I was in Boston, we were already meeting . . .

You were meeting as the collective by then?

Yeah, well, we weren't calling ourselves that.

Ah, I see.

That was sort of a transitional period. But definitely during the time period that I was here in Boston, we were meeting—I remember sometimes we would have meetings outdoors by the river in the summertime. And at the same time we were meeting, I was working in effect in women's health. And the first assignment that I had was—there was a hospital at that time that was called Boston City Hospital, and it was sort of the hospital for poor people in Boston, run by the city. The resource of last resort. All kinds of poverty. All kinds of just what life imposes on poor people and people of color. Not that all of their patients were people of color, but pretty much all of them were poor. I can guarantee you that.

It has since sort of been reformed as something called Boston Medical Center, with a lot of the same clientele, but it also has sort of upped its view—not its view of itself, but its purpose. So it is in fact the medical center, but it's the medical center that's still affiliated with the city of Boston and with BU Medical School, and they still have that commitment of serving people without any other resource.

But at the time I was working there, it was kind of—it did not really have the reputation it has since formed, because it was just seen as that poor person's hospital. I don't know whether you ever watched a series called *St. Elsewhere*. It was set in Boston, in the hospital that was pretty much like I described. And the people here in Boston particularly used to call Boston City "the real *St. Elsewhere*."

Did this experience influence your own particular involvement with Combahee?

Well, I was seeing all kinds of things in my work. I did contraceptive counseling. And we saw, us counselors—there were three of us that were counselors in this clinic—we were sited at Boston City. All the other sites for this program where they provided services were at neighborhood health centers. But we were at the epicenter, because not only were we at Boston City, but unlike other sites—usually they had like one or two sessions a week. We had two sessions a day. So we were doing like ten sessions of family planning counseling. In other words, a morning session, an afternoon session, five days a week.

The volume was very large. I was seeing a lot of stuff. And I was seeing, you know, very young girls who were sexually active or becoming sexually active. I was seeing teenagers. I was also seeing women who occasionally told me about being battered. There was nowhere to send them. And I would go to our meetings and I would say, you know, "I was in the clinic today and I met this woman who was telling me about how her partner was burning her with cigarettes, and I had nowhere to refer her to." Because I knew there was no one there.

So I mean, it sort of made real my understanding of what was happening to women in the context of healthcare. The other thing I did during that period is that there was a feminist health center— they were already open and providing healthcare but they were pretty new, and so I made it my business to make contact with people at the feminist health center, and that was the beginning of a very long-term relationship with them over the years.

Why do you guys ultimately then decide to form this separate organization?

As I said, I can't remember whether Demita went to that conference in Detroit. I know my sister did. I know she wasn't thrilled with what happened there.

And I think there were some other things, other interactions she had had with people with NBFO. They were not helpful. I suspect that one thing that might have happened is Barbara got in touch with them and said—I almost remember either she wrote something on this, or said something like, "Okay, so all these women got together in New York. And are you going to do anything with that? Are you going to do that as a basis for organizing?"

The other thing you should know, because I think this relates too, is that there was a time period, after the summer of '75, in the fall of '75, when I appear in Boston, Barbara got a job working at a national newspaper in Washington, DC. So she moved to Washington. The important thing I wanted to tell you is that because Barbara went to DC, she had the opportunity of connecting with women from DC who were also involved in the NBFO. So she had exposure to sort of several different sites.

Right. Well, what was your experience in writing the statement?

Well, I think what happened is that Barbara met a woman who was on the faculty at Ithaca College. Her name was Zillah Eisenstein. One thing you should understand is that—and this is still true, and it was true then—is that Barbara was like the liaison or the face of the Black feminist organizing effort here. And so Zillah was not going to contact me. Zillah didn't know from me. There was a socialist feminist conference I think, that was mentioned in the statement, at Antioch [College] in Yellow Springs, I guess, Ohio.

And so Zillah asked Barbara at a certain point if we could write a statement about our politics. At the time that we wrote the statement, it was just my sister, myself, and Demita, just the three of us. But with that invitation, we were very interested in pursuing it.

**What about the politics of it [do] you think were import-
ant and significant?**

Two things I want to say about that. One is that from the time I
started meeting with folks from Boston—that would have been
the summer of '75 on—we were discussing our politics and developing our politics. We were sharing readings with each other, and
doing some political work as well, because there were things that
happened.

There were some cases having to do with abortion rights. One
involved a Black doctor at Boston City Hospital, the place that I
mentioned. I had some contact with him when I was there. Not
around his case, but he was being accused of performing an abortion where the baby was alive, I guess, post-abortion. And so he
was up on some very serious charges. He was acquitted. But we
were doing political work to support him.

So we were both discussing and developing our political concepts in those meetings, including the ones I mentioned by the river, and also getting involved in some political activities. In terms
of developing our politics, I think one of the biggest emphases for
us is that we were familiar enough with the women's movement
and feminist analysis and ideology by the time we started talking
with each other to know that our realities as Black women were
not being addressed. And so, we kind of knew what was there
in a way. And we had read it. We had had interactions with people, more or less. Other feminists who were white. Racism—addressing racism, and probably class, really, when we think about
it, were two sort of missing-in-action pieces that we knew were
very important.

I guess what I'm trying to say is that when we sat down to
write the statement, there was a lot of material ideally that we had

already covered in terms of discussion, and in terms of experience, and in terms of reading or studying, that put us in a position to develop our own analysis.

In reference to that, what do you think the significance of your contribution to Black feminism politically is then?

Number one, we were proof positive that there was such a thing as a Black woman who was committed to feminism, or Black women who were committed to feminism. Plural, more than one. We also contributed the fact that for some of us—that is to say—feminists were not white. That we had to include all of our identities and experiences. And so for us, that meant dealing with racism was not optional. It wasn't like, "Oh, well, we feel like we're on the left, or feminists are on the left, and so, you know, we probably should look at racism, or we probably should look at class." We had been incredibly affected by both phenomena—in my case, long before I realized that I also was dealing with sexism. So there was no way that even with our commitments to feminism we could leave our other experiences and our conditions and status behind.

So what we did, which I think is a tremendous contribution to politics in general, is that we really worked and struggled to develop a political analysis that took into account the multifaceted aspects of our identities and of our conditions. And I think the reason I say that it was such a contribution in general is because when I think about the approaches toward certain oppressions or whatever you want to call them—for example, if someone's a socialist, it's only about economics. It's only about work. It's only about material conditions. It's only about capitalism. And it's often only about men.

And so that is to some extent—as important as all those things are, that's kind of a flat slice, when you think of it. Or a thin slice, because as difficult as all those things I laid out are, for us, there's even more going on than that. Because, yes, the workplace, we deal with many, many things that are characteristic of what happens with workers who are oppressed. You know, low wages, unsafe working conditions, et cetera. But we also deal with low wages because we're female. And we deal with conditions of employment that include sexual harassment in a way that men do not and have not experienced, particularly before a certain point.

When the time comes that some men in fact have women who are supervising them, then that is perhaps the possibility more of sexual harassment going the other way. That it's toward men. But the thing is, [laugh] because of the standard operating procedure in the workplace and the context of patriarchy, most bosses up to a certain point, even today, are men. And so what that puts us in jeopardy of is sexual harassment.

And then add to it, [laugh] and I know you know this is true, but then add to it to the fact that not only are we female and therefore subject to or at risk for sexual harassment, but we are Black females. And so what that means is that because we're Black, then the way that we are seen in terms of our sexuality, our morals, our [so-called] sorry history of immorality, however you want to put it, that then even intensifies the risk.

So I feel like what we contributed was a politics that says, "No, it is not as simple-minded and flat and one-dimensional as you all may think it is." And you can look at many different identities or conditions. You can look at many of those. For example, I was focusing on people in the workplace. Workers' oppression. I was talking about it in terms of women, and then in terms of

Black women. Well, there's something else I had thought of. We can just take it into another arena. Health care is a perfect arena, because while white women had a ton of stuff to deal with in relationship to getting healthcare and medical care as females, we had all of that too, and then we had the things that were sort of attendant again on our Black identities and our identities as women of color.

So while white women were being treated in wildly sexist ways and wildly disrespectful ways to them as females, they encountered almost inevitably male doctors and male providers at that time. I tell you that because you know, we're all at risk. Women are more at risk in general, too, I think from bad treatment in the context of mental illness, psychiatry. And one of the big contributors to that was Freud, and his theory, because we were all hysterical or you know, I won't say "we," because he surely wasn't thinking of us, but women—women were hysterics, and neurotic, et cetera, et cetera. But the thing is, I believe when you get—when Black women are involved, whatever is happening to people who share parts of our identity, it goes farther.

How do you think the Combahee statement and the collective's contributions to Black feminism hold up over time? What I mean is that today we have women like Oprah Winfrey, Michelle Obama, and other wealthy, high-profile Black women who are often sort of held up as a barometer of progress in American society.

Archetypes.

Exactly. So I'm wondering how you think that the theories and the ideas that were developed in the Combahee

**River Collective Statement make sense of the world that
we live in today, given those new realities.**

I think they really hold up, because first of all, most people are
not living the lives of Oprah and Michelle. I can't speak about
Oprah, but my sense of Michelle is that—sort of knowing the
places where she's been, the fact that she's a lawyer, the fact that
at a certain point she worked at the University of Chicago Medical
Center, and, if I'm not mistaken, she was involved with community relations.

Well, the last job I had in health care, I worked at a children's
hospital called the Floating Hospital for Children, and it's a part of
Tufts Medical Center. I worked as I said at the pediatric hospital,
[and] there was a woman who was hired relatively shortly after I
came there, by my boss. And basically her job was—when I heard
what Michelle had been doing at the University of Chicago hospital, I thought, "This sounds so much like this position that my
boss created."

And our case, at Tufts—most of the medical center is located in the heart of Chinatown. There's always been—a conflicting
relationship, a David and Goliath kind of thing—because here you
have all these people, poor people of color, because most of the
people who live in Chinatown are not well off.

And so the community was always, or at least potentially at
loggerheads with the medical center, because the medical center
was huge and rich and ate a lot of geography. [laugh] And could buy
a lot of geography. But the point I wanted to make is that knowing
that Michelle did that, that that was her job, and knowing that also
she was involved in law, I know she came up against sexism and
discrimination and whatever, as a female as well as a Black person.
I suspect—and this is because I have more of a concept of what Mi-

chelle is like, rather than Oprah, who is just in another realm than I am—that she was quite aware of feminist issues, and dealt with them in the process of doing her work and living her life.

And what I think the Combahee River [Collective] Statement did, and I sort of want to go back to when it was newer, is that I think it must have given a lot of Black women literally like a hand-hold. Something that exists in reality, in black and white literally, that they could read, hold on to, and say "Oh, yes, I experienced that too. I've had these kinds of issues and conflicts and difficulties too."

So I guess what I'm saying, to go back to the statement, the ideas that we developed—that that probably helped to foster the development of Black feminism, and that it continues.

You know, one of the things that amazes me still is that my awareness at this point—and when I say this point, like let's say the last five or ten years, or fifteen years—how many Black women there are now who say, "Oh yes, I'm a feminist. We're feminists." And like not bat an eye. There was a time when that was like really, really uncommon. Really embattled. To say that you were a feminist—you were in a very embattled position.

There's one more piece I want to talk about in terms of that, too, and it has specifically to do with the fact that our collective was located in Boston. I haven't been involved in any organizing specifically focusing on Black feminism for some time. I heard a Black woman, who is relatively new of the Boston chapter of the NAACP, talk about the women's march [January 21, 2017], and wondering what her individual decision was going to be in relationship to the march. Then she said, "Then they invited me to speak." [laugh] And she said, "Then I really had to think about how am I seeing this." And she brought up some of the same kinds of issues that I was kind of referring to, that we dealt with back in the day. You know, should Black women be committed to feminism? Are our needs being met? And what it made me think of, hearing her talk, and just realizing in general that this was an issue I suspect that came up nationally around that women's march, I thought, you know, "Well, Boston was different." Because we were here.

We [Combahee] had a tremendous influence and effect, I think, on the rest of the women's movement here. And what I'm talking about is that unlike maybe in other places where the feminist movements of course existed—because they existed all over this country and they were quite strong—but here in Boston, the many, many white women of many stripes of feminist knew to a certainty that there were Black women who were feminists, who were activists, who were with them together on whatever march or picket lines or whatever we were doing, but also that we were Black women who were holding the movement, including them, accountable for issues to do with race and racism. And then just access.

There's a minister who I heard speak earlier this year, and I very much admire him. He is a retired or emeritus UU [Unitarian Universalist] minister. He's a Black man. He is wonderful. I happened to hear a sermon that he gave at a UU church, which was broadcast on the radio. That whole speech was about who are you—who do you know? As his example, he was talking about the march in Selma, and how after Bloody Sunday, when the first people who made the first attempt were beaten so horribly and attacked so horribly, that King put out the call to clergy all over this country, to come and support.

The point he was making that in terms of the Unitarians, the Unitarian Universalists at that time, there were a lot of folks in this predominantly white denomination who nevertheless had had real contact and real relationships, for various reasons of various sorts, with Black people. And his point was, he said, "Yes, why did people go to Selma?" Yes, it was a righteous cause. You know, it was because of how important the cause was, and how compelling it was. But he said, also, it was because these people were connected to each other in different ways. For example, there was some UU person King had invited to Ghana when they had their celebration for the beginning of the nation. And he went with a white Unitarian Universalist. I don't remember the name, but the thing is, is that these—King and this white guy from the UU went. That's just one example of the connections they had.

I feel here in Boston, those kind of relationships were possible and happened, as opposed to some other places where people— perhaps white people were concerned about racism and did what they could, but there were no bodies. I shouldn't say there were no bodies, but see, we had a very strong entity, and we had a strong presence. People knew we existed because of the statement. I can think of a lot of activities and activism that we were involved in that we either drew white women into, because they [needed] to be there, too, or vice versa.

There was an active connection then among different feminist groups, and one of them were Black [women]. And the other piece that occurs to me is that we also drew many women of color who were not Black to us. We had connections with Latinas. We had connections with Asian women. We did draw women of color, and I'm so glad. And they drew us too. Because it wasn't just like one way. When we'd find out about things that were happening, we would get ourselves there as well. I just think it's really important to have that piece, because it wasn't just that we were connecting with white women. We were connecting with all kinds of women. I'm thinking of—there was a time period in the late seventies where we had a series of murders of Black women [in Boston].

We put out a pamphlet about what was happening, and included in it were some ideas about how women could protect themselves. One of the reasons Barbara thought to write it, and we thought it was important, was because, at first, these murders understandably were addressed in the Black community, but the approach was very sort of male-oriented, and their notion was like, you know, "We Black men have to protect our Black women."

Well, that's all well and good, but one of the things Barbara and us realized was that all women did not have the access to being protected by a Black man, and all women don't want that. And so what we did is we came up with some suggestions about how one might protect oneself and be careful and mindful, without necessarily only having a Black man to depend on. And every time we put out that pamphlet, we had to increase the number of Black women who had died.

I'm thinking of a demonstration that was organized in the Black community. But that a lot of women from the feminist community—so there were white women there, but I was particularly thinking of a woman who we were connected with, who's Latina. You have this photograph and you can see a lot of people in the crowd, individually. And it's a very diverse group of folks and, again, as far as I'm concerned, that might not have looked that way if it hadn't been for our collective being here. And it was both a matter of relationships—you know, connections and relationships with these women. One of my best friends at the time is very clearly pictured in the march. But also because of our being around, their consciousness was raised. So when these white women on their phone heard about the terrible news about what was happening with Black women being murdered, they knew. They knew to be there. We didn't have to tell them. We didn't have to invite them. We didn't have to call them up and say, like, you know, "We really think you should get yourselves out here for this demonstration."

There were people there who had not—"consciousness-raising" [is] not exactly the word I'm looking for. There were women there who were there because they had been touched by the work that we and other Black women had done. So as I said, I just feel like the situation in Boston was a little different because we were there.

DEMITA FRAZIER

KEEANGA-YAMAHTTA TAYLOR: To begin with, when did you begin to start identifying as a feminist?

DEMITA FRAZIER: This question is so interesting to me because I did not have a word for the way I was feeling, or my thoughts, but when I was sixteen, I left high school after being involved in the antiwar effort at my high school, and being essentially one of a handful of students of color who were sent back to their home high schools for being seditious, basically. So in Chicago—this is post-*Brown*, so this is ten years after *Brown v. Board of Education*. Chicago, I guess, was finally getting around—and I think two classes before mine—so the eighth-grade graduating class of '64—and maybe going back as far as '62—there was this program that they created—the board of education created the permissive transfer program. And this was set up to desegregate the—for all intents and purposes—we took a test. It was a citywide test, and it was like the Boston Latin test. If you passed the test, you would be permitted to transfer out of your neighborhood Black school— your neighborhood Black middle-class school, by the way—and go to the white upper-middle-class and upper-class schools on the North Side. You know, Chicago is a pretty segregated town. So, this meant going to schools in areas that were completely foreign and new to me. So through the permissive transfer program, I got accepted in four, and chose Nicholas Senn.

And why did you choose Senn?

I don't know. I can't remember. I think—I want to say it was because of two things. They had a very strong music program. They were known in the city as having won all these choral competitions. They had a full orchestra. A full band. And they also had a very, very strong academic status—I would have to say it was like a Boston Latin, in that like 99 percent of the students who graduated were accepted into college. And it was in Rogers Park, which was, at that time one, of the largest concentrations, outside of New York, of Holocaust survivors. So the heavily Jewish community. And for African American people, that awareness that these people had survived so much—knowing that these are smart people and they, like us, really cared about their children's education and about their school—that was another reason why I'm pretty sure my family was—not my family, but I think my mom—and I don't—you can't quote her because she's dead, but I'm pretty sure it was—all of that was in the mix. Also, from my grammar school, I think there was a cohort of the graduating class, probably a cohort of more than twenty-five of the hundred of us, who were accepted in these fancy schools. My elementary school, Park Manor, was firmly in the Black lower middle class, with a good teaching staff and a solid administration—was kind of you know—did you read the book, by the way, *Negroland* by Margo Jefferson?

No.

You should—I mean, I would invite you to read that, because it provides a really good background on the Negrotocracy [laugh] of Chicago. Prior to attending the University of Chicago Lab School, Margo went to Park Manor.

Ah. Yes, yes, yes. Okay.

And her family was in Park Manor a generation before me.

So I came at the tail end of—the Park Manor school had a wonderful reputation in the Black middle class, and it was a feeder school for them into the lab school. Into where she and her sister went.

University of Chicago—the laboratory school. In any event, [laugh] so that's how I ended up at Senn. For two tumultuous years.

So yeah, for two tumultuous years. And what happened? Did you end up going back to your home school?

Well, I was kind of kicked out because I was part of a group of students who organized a walkout in protest of the Vietnam War. This Black judge here in Boston—who was from Chicago, who also was a permissive transfer student—he and I didn't know each other until I began doing training for the trial court here in Massachusetts on diversity. And Judge King, who—we were talking over lunch, and we discovered we were both from Chicago, and contemporaries, and went to—he went to Schurz. I went to Senn. He said, "Well, you know, we weren't meant to survive in those schools. You do know that, right?" And it all came back to me. Because I actually had a nervous breakdown. Alone, by myself, isolated, both by my family and by the school. It was actually a nervous *breakthrough*, as I described it later. But it was a very intense experience that I also must say I would not have traded for anything in the world. Nothing. I discovered things about myself through the experience that

I would never have learned in the same way had I gone back to my high school, which, once I was kicked out of Senn, I did, where I was one of six students in the only AP classes offered in every subject. There were six of us, and we just went as a cohort from class to class to class to class, all day long. In our own little private—mini private school at Parker High School. So, yeah, and I dropped out after six months and just, you know, went my merry way.

From age fourteen to sixteen, I began to understand that I was going to be a political person because I was interested in what was going on in civil rights, with the antiwar movement, and because I was—many of us who were high school students during that time period, who were alleged to be high achieving or exceptionally bright, were being courted by all the upper-class schools—the Harvards and the Radcliffes, et cetera.

And I was acutely aware, for a lot of reasons, of how class was starting to have a really big impact on my life. More than it did when I was just the marginal-class girl in the Black middle-class neighborhood. That's where I really learned about class. But I began investigating political ideas at fourteen and fifteen. I started reading Baldwin by mistake when I was fifteen. I found a book on a friend's father's nightstand and basically stole it and read it, and I was like, who is this?

What year was this?

1967, '68, '69 were the years of my political awakening.

Wow. That's a hell of a time to have a political awakening! [laugh]

So going back, when I was sixteen, I was living away from home. I had escaped my family, and in the midst of some of the political organizing that was going on at the University of Chicago. I walked into a meeting, and this is what's odd. I don't think of myself as Zelig. Do you know the movie *Zelig*?

Mm-hmm.

The stupid Woody Allen movie? Where the character appears in the background of all these very important political events? I happened to be roommates with somebody who was deeply involved with the case of a socialist woman at the University of Chicago who was denied tenure. And so when this woman was denied tenure, there was a huge meeting that was being called, and I went with my housemate.

And I sat on the fringe of this group, and I happened to turn and look down to my right, and there was a book. A very thin paperback book. And on the front cover was a symbol I had never seen before, except in astrology. It was a woman symbol—the symbol for Venus—with a black fist in the middle. And it was called *Woman Power*, by a woman named Celestine Ware. You ever heard of her?

No.

Celestine Ware was an African American woman who wrote this book, *Woman Power*. Had to have been published in '68 or maybe '69. '68 probably, because it was a paperback.

I basically stumbled on this book, but when I sat there and started leafing through it, I immediately knew I was a feminist. I was like, "Oh, that's what I am! [laugh] OK, I get it now."

Wow.

Yes. Because having been raised by a woman who did not believe in male supremacy on any level, it just wasn't real—and then having a mother who had escaped Mississippi, with this part of her soul intact—my mother was not interested in studying white people. She didn't think they were superior in any way. She couldn't understand—she said, "Don't believe the hype. I don't know where they got that. They're not supreme in anything. That's that."

[laugh]

And the way she said stuff to me sometimes, I'd be like, "Okay, all right. Well, all right, that's truth right there." So I was raised—and it wasn't that that was the complete story, because she was also a child of Mississippi. So believe me when I tell you, things came out of her mouth that were—I look back and I'm thinking, "That wasn't helpful." Some of the sexist stuff, some of the stuff based in the worst of religiosity, even though she was not a Christian herself. But you know what I'm saying. It's like there [was] always a mixed story. But the dominant story that I got, that I took to heart, had to do with the myth of supremacy.

So I count—looking at that book, just looking down to my right, it was amazing! It was just there on the radiator cover that I was sitting on. It was a very cold day, and it was a very cold room. I remember thinking, that's me. And I stole the book, of course, and then took it home and read the entire thing. And that sort of—that was the winter of 1969, so from that point on, I knew I was a feminist. Hadn't thought about being a Black feminist, and I didn't even know that Celestine Ware was Black. I didn't find that out until later.

But her message was very clear. It was wonderful. And that was another thing, why I also didn't have any compunction or fear about defining myself as a Black feminist, because when I think about my feminist antecedents, and I think about the covert ways in which African American women have had to communicate to their daughters and . . . you know, their children—the strongest messages about not being like white people, and not being a woman in the same vein that women were being talked about—that was considered strength in my family. Even though my mother would still say things like, you know, you have to be—try to be—feminine. Try that. But it wasn't like you had to be that.

Let me just ask you, when you said that as soon as you read the book, you understood that you were a feminist, what was in it that made that connection for you?

There were three things about the book that really struck me. First of all, it was an analysis of my position as a Black woman. To be honest, it was one of those things where I read the entire book, and feel like I imprinted what she said, but I don't remember quotes or particular things that she said.

But it was this analysis of our condition. Recognizing sexism, recognizing heteropatriarchy. Recognizing the right and the responsibility of us to analyze our position as [women as] a part of our radical perspective. It was required. It wasn't that you shouldn't be analyzing, nor was it race versus gender.

And then the other thing that really stood out was it was unapologetic. Because I was—I felt unapologetic. I was really clear that I had a right to investigate my personal power. And that's what I wanted to say to you, Keeanga. I was obsessed with the idea of what it means to be empowered. I felt keenly as a child that there were so many out-of-control adults in my life who were just disappointing [laugh] on so many levels with regard to their own adulthood and their ability to take care of children and all of that.

So, obviously the period that you're talking about—'67, '68, and '69—[was] an incredibly politically volatile moment in American history.

Right.

What were you doing at this time? What were you involved with?

That's a very good question. I can tell you. So I would have graduated—I was supposed to graduate in 1970 from high school. And I left high school, as I told you, because of some antiwar activities I got involved with. I actually decided in the fall of 1969, once I had left my high school, gone back to my local high school, that I was still restless. I had investigated the Young Socialist Alliance (YSA), but it was too white, and too problematic on other levels. So I was like, "Okay fine." I took the books, I took the reading lists, and I moved on.

[YSA was] really problematic in terms of how it felt—I couldn't get questions answered. That's always been an issue for me. If you can't answer my questions, I'm really—I'm done. Because I have a need to know. In any event, I got involved with the Black Panther breakfast program through a friend.

Really!

And did that for a month, and as it stands, it was right before Thanksgiving until right when Fred Hampton was murdered.*

And the ironic thing, and I should mention this to you—another one of those Zelig effects of my life—I had been involved with

---

* Fred Hampton, the chairman of the Illinois chapter of the Black Panther Party, was murdered in his bed on December 4, 1969, shot and killed by the Chicago Police Department with the aid of the FBI's COINTELPRO (counterintelligence program).

the program since I think end of September, but it really started going at the end of October. And I was getting constantly macked by the men. I'm a sexual abuse survivor, and I really just was not having it. Really. I mean, I look back on myself, and I think, god, I was really on fire. Because I didn't even—I was just so upset that I couldn't be taken seriously as a committed activist—it seemed like no matter what I did, the first thing that these men were dealing with was like trying to mack me. I'm here for a political reason and you're trying to—oh!

It brings up a lot of anger all over again. Because it was again another indicator that I was on the right track with regard to inquiring, why does sexism always impede my ability to manifest my own personal power? Why? Why, why, why? So Fred Hampton, in fact, happened to come by the building that day when we were packing food. You know, packing the lunch bags. And he was so chill and so kind and so non-macking. I never forgot that.

And then he was killed the next day.

Oh, my god.

Yes. It was really—'68 and '69, I mean, I don't know how we all got through that. I really don't. So I guess I'm going to say to you, I did that briefly, but then realized I just needed to get out of that situation. So I began to work with people in the antiwar movement more actively. And I studied lithography one summer, at the Art Institute of Chicago. So I began working with a couple of artists to do poster-making. And I don't know if you know this, but Chicago is actually one of the capitals—in the 1940s through the 1970s— one of the capitals of lithography and printing in this country.

I didn't know that.

Many of the posters we made ended up in museums because they were real artifacts of that movement and beautifully made, et cetera, et cetera. So I learned all about lithography and what it meant to do artistic activism; during that time I was also developing my understanding of being disciplined, meeting deadlines, and just got a lot of exposure to the strains of thought around the left during that time. I would go anywhere to hear people talk or speak, and I never felt any fear of being the one Black person by myself. I just never did.

I was spending most of that time reading. Once I dropped out of high school, I continued my own self-education, because I had learned that I was an autodidact. I really had a need to continue to be engaged intellectually. So I just continued doing what I normally did, which was go to the public library and read, constantly, all day, all the time. So let's see. Antiwar movement. Then I also got involved toward the end of 1971—I went away to Bennington with my girlfriend at the time. We didn't know we were girlfriends—oh!

I was at Bennington, just for a semester, came back to Chicago, and then got re-involved in the reproductive rights movement. Because briefly, when the Jane Collective had started expanding, doing more outreach to women of color, and helping more women of color obtain what were at the time illegal abortions, I really was drawn to what they were doing.

And it was interesting because one of the things about me and Barbara, I would suspect, and other women in Combahee as political operatives and organizers, is that the fact that we were women who were at the time either queer or lesbian did not impact in any way our decision to be involved in reproductive rights.

It's interesting because we never actually, as far as I can tell, as far as the classic definition, really practiced what people now call identity politics. Because the centerpiece and the center focus was not an aspect of our identity, but the totality of what it meant to be a Black woman in the diaspora. Which also created both some very negative and positive interactions and interchanges over the years for us.

Let me ask you to go back and say a few words about what the Jane Collective was.

It was a collective of women who decided to organize around helping women interrupt pregnancies through abortion, primarily. And what they did is they had a network of medical providers who were anonymous but who were physicians and I think nursing—nurse practitioners (though they wouldn't have been called that then) who helped women.

It was an underground movement to help women gain access to abortion. And at the time that they were operating, the Illinois Women's Abortion Access Coalition was formed and began to help to bring pressure again—bring pressure in the courts, which led to *Roe v. Wade*.

Why was abortion such a focal point for women's activism at this time? Because Barbara talks a lot about this—she told me about abortion rights organizing in Boston and Cambridge.

That's right.

You're saying the same kind of phenomenon is happening in Chicago. So why is abortion rights such a focal point of organizing?

Well, the whole notion of reproductive rights was core to the early feminist enterprise. The ability to have agency over your body. The ability to not be dead in a fucking back alley because you need to interrupt a pregnancy, and it's your damn body. Why can't you do what you want with it?

So it was coming—and don't forget, we're talking about a movement that also was—I'm going to say *incubated* in the minds and hearts of frustrated older women. The influx of young women who were at that point in childbearing years and were dealing with the real implications of what it meant when you did not have control over your body—you had that coming together of those different influences that caused reproductive rights to be so important. Does that make sense?

Absolutely.

I think the Afrofuturists are right—the whole notion about both being in your body and escaping your body. Having control of your body and having a sense of your destiny about your body—all of that I think comes together at different times in history.

And I think in our so-called second wave of feminism—it came together around the issue of sexuality, sexual openness, sexual agency, and agency over the body. And I just thought about this just now [laugh]. It just came to me just now that that's what was going on. There's more too. Don't forget, this is a time when we were uncovering sterilization abuse against women of color—Native American, African American, poor white women, Latina women. This is suddenly coming to the surface. At the same time, we're also really dealing with the Tuskegee experiment. And we weren't aware of Henrietta Lacks at that point, even though that was happening in the '50s and '60s. But you see what I'm saying.

There was a whole lot of suddenly emerging information about the way that the state and the heteropatriarchal state had controlled and limited women's agency through their bodies.

That's really important. Then what is the—if this is happening in the feminist movement, then why—why Black feminism?

Yes, Okay! [laugh] I get to talk about the intersection.

Yes.

I have to talk to the young woman—Kimberlé Crenshaw . . . who says that she coined the term *intersectionality*. I always laugh when I read that because I remember the day we were sitting at the women's center in Cambridge, drafting our probably third or fourth draft of the statement, I said, "You know, we stand at the intersection where our identities are indivisible." There is no separation. We are as Black women truly and completely intact in our paradox, and there's nothing paradoxical about oppression [laugh]. There's nothing paradoxical about it.

And I remember clearly, I said something about this white man as I'm walking down Dorchester Avenue—this is going in my annals of racism—in broad daylight, yells across the street at me—I'm like twenty-five years old—"Hey, black pussy! You want to suck my dick?"

And I, you know, thank god I'm Jackie's child, because I looked across the street and I thought, "What's this? Oh my god! What depravity is this?" [laugh] I didn't feel a sense of shame or anything. I'm thinking, "White people, what's wrong with you?"

Right. [laugh]

And there's not a Black man who will ever have that experience, because Black and pussy together—you can't break that apart.

[laugh]

You feel me? [laugh] I know Barbara must have mentioned to you what a wild card I am. Sincerely, to make comedy. Comedy will save us all.

So, honestly, I never, and we never, and I can say this—I feel like I can say this and not feel any other way about it—one of the things about me and Barbara and Beverly and the women who were organizing the National Black Feminist Organization (NBFO), which became Combahee, was that there was never a conflict in us. That was what drew us to one another, is that we recognized inherently that there was no conflict. That that was manufactured. And that we in ourselves, in our very bodies, represented another sort of emerging understanding of the complexity of the politics.

Right.

You understand what I'm saying? So it's like, we knew it. It was nascent. We knew it—and we weren't willing to let it go. Why Black feminism? We had to create Black feminism. We had to actually create it. But I think what I feel honestly is that we—it's almost as if we were graced by the universe with timing, and positioning, to be just at that moment ready to take up a mantle that had been there and had been carried by other women. That's what we said.

You know, we are the daughters of Ida B. Wells. We're the daughters of every Black woman who has been a leader—Sojourner Truth, Harriet Tubman, and all the millions of unnamed warriors. All the millions of unnamed ones. We are in a long line. We're just calling it—we're calling it what it is now—Black feminism is a representation of Black women's power. Black women's agency. Black women's right to look at their material conditions, analyze it, interrogate it, and come away with an analysis that's about empowerment. That's why. [laugh] We had to.

Could you say something about what you think were the limits of what is now understood to be second-wave feminism?

Oh yeah [laugh]. The same damn limits that occur in this settler colony we live in. The simple limits that have always been in place. The nihilistic sickness of white supremacy. I'll never forget recognizing back in . . . I think it was 1975 . . . white women aren't going to readily deal with their racism, as feminists. They aren't going to deal with it. They really aren't gonna. I mean, there were people, as you know, who were socialist feminists, who talked about the issue of race, and there were feminists who were—radical feminists who I think were beginning to address the issues of class and race in feminism.

But in terms of the quote mainstream close quote feminist movement, every other movement in this country that's fueled by white folks' energy, the one thing we are not going to talk about [laugh] in a real way would be race. We just can't go there. That's that third rail, so—and we knew we were on to something, because you know, people started crying everywhere we turned [laugh].

So where did the Combahee River Collective come from?

How did we evolve into that?

Yeah.

You asked do I consider myself a socialist now. And I have to say, I'd have to say yes, but with a lot of qualifications. Because now

I've lived long enough to see, we're monkeys with cell phones. On the evolutionary curve, we're so low on the evolutionary climb that not in my lifetime will we even be able to come up with a plan of how to get to a more equitable socialist life in late-stage capitalism. It's just really not happening. However, I'm still dedicated to the principles and precepts. Definitely.

Now, Combahee evolved out of the National Black Feminist Organization. At the time that I met Barbara, I had moved from Chicago to Boston, and had begun the Boston chapter of the National Black Feminist Organization, which was founded by a group of very odd and interesting people—women from the Black church, Black Democratic politicians, and then a handful of rough-housing lesbians.

[laugh]

For real. It was crazy. Margaret Sloan—who introduced me to Gloria Steinem, okay—Margaret used to travel around with Gloria and do all the early feminist roadshows. That was actually prior to the beginning of *Ms.* magazine. So I was living with Margaret, her partner at the time, and their child in Chicago. When I moved to Boston, Margaret had moved to New York and had begun with these women. Margaret was a lesbian and had begun organizing the National Black Feminist Organization. It had a platform. It was a very conservative platform from our perspective. And after we had been a member group for a year and a half, by June of '76, we had decided to break off because we considered ourselves radical, socialist, and working in a collective style, not in a hierarchical style. And then Barbara, inveterate historian that she is, came to a meeting, and very excitedly, told us about the story of the successful escape of a number of enslaved people at the Combahee River, led by Harriet Tubman, and that's how we got the name. Of course, this is all pre-Google. Every-thing's so much easier now. So much easier. But Barbara had come across in her reading information about Harriet Tubman leading the slave revolt that took place at the Combahee River.

So we evolved out of the National Black Feminist Organiza-tion, and, once we began meeting and talking, realized we were more radical, and we were wanting a different kind of structure. And we wanted to have an economic analysis as well. We weren't willing to just have a discussion about, you know, sort of fitting into mainstream capitalist thinking.

One of things that really stood out was that we had an analy-sis that NBFO did not. We had an economic analysis. Because we were all either nascent or just fully blown out-and-about socialists. And whether we were democratic socialists—whatever flavor you choose to apply to it—we were very clear that taking collective action was important, having an economic analysis was import-ant. Understanding—and by the way, some of us were second- or third-generation union babies. So we had mom and dads, or moms, who were in unions. And that was certainly true for me, and that left a lasting impression on me. Because my mother was a person who didn't even believe in voting, but she believed in the union. Because that was on the ground. She could see what happened when she showed up, as opposed to dropping your vote in the void.

Where did the statement come from, and why?

How did we decide to even write the statement?

Yeah.

Well, if you remember, in the '60s and '70s, statement writing was a big deal [laugh]. There were a lot of intellectual and philosophical beachheads being established. And we decided to write because we had been running consciousness-raising groups for many years, when we were meeting at the Women's Center, and we were accumulating a lot of data from Black women in the diaspora. We were getting all sorts of women coming through. I mean, hundreds and hundreds of Black women. Unbelievable.

So we had lots of women—we got a lot of input from women about wanting to know more about what we did. And Barbara's a writer. At the time, I was a deeply closeted writer. Beverly is also an intellectual and a writer. So we just, you know, it became what we did.

There was also the reality of white feminism. It became important for us to establish what we considered to be our Black feminist theory because we did a lot of coalition work and believed deeply in building coalitions to do the work necessary to destroy white supremacy. We wanted to speak in our own voice, as Black feminists.

And in doing that work, of course, we were surfacing all manners of racism and craziness on the part of working with these white women. So it was important for us to put out to the larger Black women's world who we were and what we were about. And to see if other women would cohere and agree. Because there was no guarantee—absolutely none—you know, we could be speaking into the void, for all we knew.

And in fact, we learned very quickly after writing the statement and continuing to organize—what we were up against was pretty daunting, because nobody had love for us [laugh]. For real. [laugh] No, really, we were troublemakers. We were just troublemakers, in the minds of so many. And that was never going to change, because that's what we really were, so—it was problematic on a lot of levels. And also very exhilarating and wonderful.

There seems to be a clear influence of not just radical ideas but socialist ideas in the statement.

Yes.

I'm wondering if you could talk some about the relationship between socialist ideas and Black feminism. And part of the reason I'm asking this is because I think given the popularity of Bernie Sanders, for example . . .

Mm-hmm.

. . . that there's a perception that socialism is sort of outside the realm of Black experience, and that this is just . . .

Right.

. . . something that white people engage with, and is not, you know, is not an idea that really has taken any root in the Black experience. And you know, in my book, in the final chapter of that book, I talk quite extensively about how socialist politics have always been a part of a Black radical organizing tradition.

Right.

And so that was one of the things that had always struck me about the Combahee statement, was that there's this kind of seamless discussion about socialist politics and ideas in concert with Black feminism. I'm just wondering if you could say something about that.

Well, you know, I'll say this. And then I can try to explore further.

I meant to say this earlier, I was twenty-five when we wrote that. And was still exploring. So, at twenty-five I had been exposed in eleven years, from fourteen to twenty-five, to the notion, and I had been doing a lot of reading, about notions of Black socialism—and also Black communism and Black Marxism. I was reading C. L. R. James and a variety of writers and thinkers coming out of the African diaspora who had that socialist and/or communist and/or Marxist philosophical foundation as a part of their analysis of what it means to be Black in the New World— the so-called New World.

And those ideas intrigued me, but I never ever ever would join an organization that did not have a feminist and a Black feminist analysis. Because if I can't have that conversation about how all those things intersect, and have a reasonable conversation without it turning into what it usually turns into, which is "Y'all need to go someplace, and get your mind right, because you're talking about the wrong things." That was the response by most Black men to us when we wanted to talk about issues of feminism. It was crazy. Not all but most.

So in my mind, and when I think about my own perspective and my own evolution as a thinker, one of the things that we did in Combahee that is a feature has to do with—I haven't put my finger on it—but we made a lot of assumptions about what those words meant and how they became actualized in the world.

We called ourselves a collective because, for one thing, I had moved to Boston from Chicago in a collective, in an economic collective of five women. We pooled all our money. We shared all our resources. We bought a car together. We moved together from Boston to Chicago. And we tried to live our lives in this nonhierarchical way, and we all shared what we got. So this was a radical idea in our little minds, you know.

The thing was, we knew it was important for us not just to have theory around the position of women relative to patriarchy. We had to have an economic analysis as well because that's another enormous feature. Again, you can't look at our situation, our condition, without looking at our economic and systemic relationship with the culture.

So that's where we started with that. We made a lot of assumptions and didn't really dwell on that aspect of who we were. We didn't actively continue except in the ways in which, whenever we would talk about women's situation, Black women's condition, it was always looking at the economics, the socioeconomics, the sociopolitical, et cetera.

But we did not write the statement as a Black feminist socialist tract. It was really about articulating a vision and a notion of what it meant to be a Black feminist. And that the fact that we were socialists was just because we wanted to have an inclusive notion about what we're talking about. We're talking about not just bras. We're talking about actual economic conditions. We're talking about history. We're talking about an array of factors that impact Black women's lives.

Let me just ask you, what do you think is the significance of the experience of the collective, the Combahee statement in general, forty years later?

Well, you know, it's way too big, because the thing is—and I can say this for myself as someone who has been pondering this—I'm writing a political biography, a political autobiography, about Combahee. And there are a lot of things about trying to sort it out, trying to sort out the lasting value, which I think is important. I think what we did in publishing that statement and then continuing to remain unapologetic Black feminists over time despite everything just really tells the story—in my mind, speaks the truth about the message that we were choosing to put out.

And there are aspects of the way we functioned as a group, as an organization, that I regret. There are ways in which we were young and naïve and just really did not invest the kind of time into looking at how we actually functioned. Somebody asked me recently, "Aren't you sad that Combahee only existed for those seven years?" And I looked at her and I thought, actually not. In those seven years, we were empowered—through our own lives and our interactions with the other sisters that came there. We can't even begin to know the impact of that experience.

What I really know is that Black feminism was a tool of empowerment that allowed the women who were participating to go out and do great things. Great, great things. Amazing things. And we were—the point wasn't about lasting and being like, you know, some groups—like NOW. Lasting forever.

Most truly radical organizations, when you're that—when you're the edge of that sword—you burn out. It's like a supernova, right? It bursts onto the scene and brings illumination. But like most things that are like that, they burn themselves out. And in the end, one of the things that I regret is that we did not have a deep, deep ongoing conversation with the African American community in Boston, so that we could continue undermining homophobia in that community and continue to ask the hard questions about class war and race war in Boston.

So there were things that we weren't able to touch on because, you know, you can only do so much. But I feel like—when I look at the work that the people who were founders of Combahee have done in their professional and personal and political lives, I have nothing but pride and a sense of humility that we didn't know it, but what we were doing was incubating the next revolution.

Mm!

Truly. I met a woman—a young Black woman at Boston University who invited me to speak at a conference told me later that her aunt in LA told her, "See, if you're a Black feminist, you can kiss having a happy life goodbye. You're never going to find a partner. You're never going to be happy because you're just always going to ask too many damn questions."

Wow.

That's a 2016 message. So Black feminism is still problematic in the Black community. And I really don't even think we have enough time to unpack who's a feminist in the Black community because Beyoncé—and see, I've got to tell you, I'm just a low-class girl from Chicago who loves to shake my butt, so part of me loves her. Part of me.

Absolutely. Yes, yes.

You understand? Come on. Beyoncé? Okay. But [laugh] there's a giant asterisk next to that. The ways in which the mainstream Black mainstream culture has just gotten into the fuckery of white mainstream culture is ridiculous. And you know what? I'm not even mad at her! Because if she wants to call herself a feminist she can do all of that. Not a problem. But don't be holding her up as the epitome.

Is there any utility in someone like Beyoncé or some of these other sort of high-profile Black women in particular, who do say that they're a feminist, as opposed to perhaps a generation ago, when everyone—kind of feminism

was just seen as something for radical women perhaps, and not something that a mainstream figure within popular culture would not only say but in many ways seem to embrace. Is there any utility in that?

Well, I would say this. I would say I will never—I'm not going to dispute Beyoncé or Solange or any of the other young sisters, including Blac Chyna [laugh]. Okay, because of the sex positivity and all that stuff. I get that too. I'm feeling them. However, what's happening is the lack of any kind of ongoing interaction about what Black feminism means. Beyoncé—well, she's an artist. So she's doing her. She's doing it the way she wants to do it. I'm not mad at her. I want to see her devote some more money to educating young Black girls. I want to see them come out and deal with the R. Kellys and the Rick Rosses of this world. . . . However, in the ways in which they can make their power meaningful, speaking out against misogynoir, speaking out and dealing with violence against African American women in the diaspora—you know what I'm saying? If they're gonna put their money behind issues that really count—I want to know about how they're doing their business. How are they paying Black people? I'm not talking about the ones in their inner circle. And all the crazy focus on the nature of Bey's and Jay's relationship? I'm feeling like this is really a generational gap for me—I don't care about their relationship. I really don't even see how people can even think that they're going to be trying to model themselves on these two. Honestly. This aspirational thing is intense! And this whole thing of making her into a goddess?

Yeah, I think there is utility. I think one of the things about age and about generational differences is that I do see that they're not performing for us, or you. In that vein, how do they use popular culture and social media as young Black feminists, and how they're thinking about Black feminism, and what they're doing with either the Combahee statement or other works by Black feminist thinkers—I mean, the statement is one thing. How do other young Black women find one another to even talk with each other about Black feminist ideology or ideas? Because this is the thing that I'm noticing. The way they talk about one another—again, part of the pornification and the spectacle—is they call each other females. Females! Like animals. I'm like, "Oh, Okay, right." And how—if I had a dollar for every young Black woman who tells me, "I don't mess with females. I don't fuck with them. All my friends are men."

What do you think is the state of Black feminism today, then?

I mean, how we understand the meaning or significance of Black feminism today, versus the kind of political tumult through which it was originally sort of articulated in the late 1960s and in the course of the '70s. Because it does seem today that there's almost a kind of respectable aspect of Black feminism that was probably unfathomable forty years ago. Michelle Obama had a conference on Black women and Black women's issues at the White House. I think it was last year. And so there's a kind of sense in which it's almost trendy to at least say that you're a feminist. Which is different from Black feminism.

But I'm just wondering how you might characterize the difference between the Black feminism from the 1960s and 1970s and what today is discussed as Black feminism.

Well, okay, three things immediately spring to mind. We've got to put things in a historical context, right? So when you think about how—Black feminism was, to me, a natural evolution for aware, progressive, Black women in the diaspora. Black feminism was a no-brainer because everything was up for question. It was the '60s. Everything was being questioned. Things were being unpacked on a very serious basis. And, radical Black thought was burgeoning. So you had—Paule Marshall came into her own during that era, right? She's going back to—right. So we're talking about a historical stream that spiked in a certain way for a certain set of reasons, in the '70s. By the way, don't forget the story of how Combahee became, was coming out of the National Black Feminist Organization, and the efforts on the part of Black women from an array of backgrounds to organize Black women in the way that NOW had been organized. Right?

But my point is, just like NOW, there have always been multiple strands to the Black feminist enterprise. There always have been. Because Black women, Black people, are as diverse as we've ever been. And you have everything from the women who were hybrids of the National Council of Negro Women—from the era of Dorothy Height, right—who were also part of NBFO. And then—and also, by the way, we had a woman in Boston—a woman from the Community Party USA who—an African American woman—who was in her forties or early fifties, when we met her. She came to my house once. I never saw her again. My point is, there have been multiple threads of Black feminist thought and practice from the beginning. But class, educational privilege, timing, a lot of factors played into whether we became salient or not. There was another Black feminist organization in Boston. I'm not sure how—whether they would describe themselves as socialists. But certainly they were Black feminists, and they did not break off from Combahee. They organized themselves separately.

But my point is, you had not just Combahee but other groups of Black women who were organizing, organizing themselves

around Black feminism, and many of them—all of them were ac-
tivist-focused. Community-activist based. Focusing on looking at
real issues affecting all Black women, which includes poor Black
women. So-called disadvantaged Black women, right? We didn't
call Black women, by the way, the Black proletariat. Just remem-
bering that so much of what brought us together was the unique
combination at that intersection of our lives, that made us demand
an analysis that incorporated the truth of what we were living and
experiencing historically and currently, and that made us uninter-
ested in adhering to what people decided was their dogma, their
theory, their whatever, if it wasn't about recognizing complexity
of the lives of Black women. And you know, we encountered everybody, from the Black Nationalists, to the DSAs, to the—you
know, everyone. No one was talking about it in the way that we
were at that moment. So that's why we stood out, I believe.

Now you see in forty years what's happened to everything.
The commodification of everything is real in late-stage capitalism. So there was always going to be a tendency, especially under
white supremacy, of elevating white women and white women's
organizations, even within the dominant culture. Because when
you think about the way Florynce Kennedy, who worked with
Gloria Steinem, was characterized in the press, and in the feminist press, versus Gloria Steinem, her sincere comrade! I mean,
I heard people in the so-called white male left, in magazines and
newspapers, refer to Florynce Kennedy as a serious bulldagger. In
her cowboy boots, her cowboy hat. Because she was deemed ec-
centric. You know her. You've seen pictures of her. And then you
have Gloria Steinem, who people never forgot that she portrayed
a Playboy Bunny. She had the inside dope on what was going on
in the Playboy hegemony. And here she is, this slender, blonde,
white woman with the long hair and the aviator glasses. And so

the point I'm trying to make is that these tropes matter. The way in which they were talked about mattered. Michele Wallace talked about this. A lot. In terms of how she was characterized as an angry Black woman. And the way Alice [Walker] was too. And the way that Toni—I mean, people didn't mess with Toni—you didn't want Toni Morrison coming for you, because [she] knows how to use her words! She can etch steel with those words. So I would say that with regard to what Black feminism looks like now and the struggle to even have an ongoing narrative about what Black feminism means—and you talked about this. I mean, the way it's been academically co-opted. And I wouldn't say co-opted if it weren't for the fact that there's still this big divide between practice and theory, right? I mean, I'm glad that the children and the young'uns are getting educated, but it looks like a factory to me right now.

Say more about that. What do you mean?

I'm thinking more about the way in which Black feminism has been—in the academy, it has been both strengthened theoretically and co-opted. And treated—I think that there's—I think when I was with the Black Women's Blueprint in Atlanta, I was really dealing with and looking at the way in which class remained an issue—"remained"—will always be a central issue for us as a people. The class divisions, with an "s." So I need to—I realize I'm—I'm feeling like more in need to interrogate that further, because that also had a role to play in terms of how Black women were able to or were not able to organize around our own issues solely, around sustaining institutions that were devoted to our survival. When you think about the institutions in this country, like the Black Women's Health Network, that's a successful organization because it saves Black women's lives, and yet Black mortality amongst mothers is as high as it has ever been. So we have impact, but it's limited. It's limited by our status. It's limited by the reality of white supremacy and then misogyny.

And how do you think the issues of class express themselves more today than they did forty years ago?

Well, first of all, I blame the *Real Housewives* and all that bullshit like *Love and Hip Hop*. I'm like, all this aspirational crap . . . that people are supposed to want and believe in because it's going to make you—what? I don't know what. So you know, supporting the beauty industry by fifty million ways—okay, fine. The shoes, the clothes, the houses, the this, the that—okay, fine, whatever. But seriously, I'm not feeling any of it. And I think that one of the things that's happened is that between organized pro-capitalist Black religion . . . not the Reverend Barbers of this world, but others who . . . are perpetuating and creating new little kingdoms for the kings, primarily, and a handful of queens. And here we are! I can't even stand it. People calling each other "queen"—it's like, "Do not call me that!" I don't—I'm not associating with royalty. So, yeah. You know, it's really—I feel like we've been—we've tricked ourselves into thinking because we moved to the suburbs and we're living in these McMansions—a handful of us, a handful of us who are associated with a certain level of class privilege in this country—that's become the dominant image.

Or maybe for always. But what I'm thinking about in terms of Black feminism and looking at how we confront late-stage capitalism, its impact, and its continuing denigration of our life, our lives. So I'm thinking, "Hmm. We can't have a conversation about democratic socialism or socialism without creating the intersection of that with class, Black women, Black feminism, the reality of Black femaleness." I mean, all of those things, right?

Yep.

For example, we're talking more and more about the need to reestablish our relationship to cooperatives. Because in fact, people of color and Black people in particular were big pioneers in the whole idea of cooperative living, because we had to [be]. True cooperatives built now, with better understanding about how we make those things work and how we make them work in spite of and on top of, or I'm not sure how to say which part of, in terms of its interaction with late-stage capitalism—how we make these structures thrive with new ideas, new notions of equity, new notions of creating the possibility of creating equitable governing and equitable governance. Ongoing education around it.

So I sort of think about Black feminist Freedom Schools that are focusing in the first three semesters on, you know, the history of cooperatives, the history of socialist thinking, how it could work for us, what are we thinking around now. When I think about Black feminism, and I think about what we bring in terms of adding to the synthesis and creation of a new hybrid like socialism—I want to build new structures that help us to get people to feel that socialism is a juicy thing. That they should be wanting this, because this really is an answer for some of our problems.

That's fantastic.

Am I making sense?

Absolutely.

One of the things that I'd like to do as we talk through in new ways about how we, as Black feminist thinkers, can continue establishing with greater clarity, our relationship to white supremacy—the way we can shift the narrative of our interaction with the dominant culture, taking more care to characterize our condition and our situation that is based on the recognition of our Black brilliance and capacity. For example, the way affirmative action doctrine is positioned—that "the improvement in our status is based on the idea that we are 'evolving' into better people because of integration," a result of closer proximity to whiteness—and that this was about us ascending to new levels of competence, when in fact what it has really been about was a very, very, very tiny developmental surge forward on the part of white people, just beginning to confront the illusion of white supremacy.

Because our competence has never been a question in my mind. Our brilliance has also never been a question. Historically proven, for many, many cultures across millennia. So it's never been about that. Characterization is indeed everything—power lies with us wrenching the narrative out of the hands that are dedicated to maintaining that illusion.

What would freedom, liberation, look like to you?

I experience a personal sense of freedom because of Black feminism, because of being a political person, I can see the impact [of] having a Black feminist analysis supports our survival as Black people as a whole. For Black women to interrogate the power dynamics in our community—I see this strengthening for Black men and boys, though they may not necessarily see that easily. And I also want to say, for me, when I think about liberation—it's becoming more and more complex to talk about it, because of the diasporic nature of our lives, right?

If we're talking simply about where we live, right here in this insanity—and I think about this in terms of the whole hemisphere, because it's so interconnected—one of the things I'm really hoping for in terms of us developing freedom has to do with our ability to really change our relationship to our genius. I can't say it any other way.

There is so much to be learned from the Brazilians and from the Afro-Brazilian experience. There's so much to be learned from us, both in every single element of our lives in the so-called United States and Canada. There's so much to be learned in terms of our sharing strategies, avenues for learning.

And so for me, freedom is really making engagement juicy and happening, so that we are able to I think synthesize some genius and find some new creativity. I also would really, really, really like it—for me freedom is getting away from this sick Mammon-driven, nihilistic bullshit we call popular culture. I'm done! I don't need my nieces to be Beyoncé. These fucking Real Housewives—I'm done. I'm done!

[laugh]

I could go on. But my point being, I'm really, really hopeful too, in terms of freedom, that we can disengage from that narrative, because again, the unquestioning assumption of that culture? No! We don't have to do that!

I'm not nostalgic. I'm looking back to mine the past for what it can help us with right now, and for what it can help us pass on and create. And I still feel part of creation. When people start talking about being an elder, I'm like, "Yeah, but you know, don't be asking about some shit that happened thirty, forty years ago." I have an eidetic memory, and I remember it exactly. But to me, that's not—I'm not nostalgic. It's like not then. What about right now? What about right now? That's me.

ALICIA GARZA

KEEANGA-YAMAHTTA TAYLOR: Next year marks the fortieth anniversary of the Combahee River Collective Statement. As you know, it was a seminal statement on the meaning and politics of Black feminism. How do you think Black feminism informs your own politics? Can you tell us also what you are trying to do with the Black Lives Matter network?

ALICIA GARZA: Just a small question. [laugh]

Just a small question. I know. I know.

Well, I mean, I'll start with how Black feminism started to influence me. Because I think it's, you know, for somebody like me, I'm reading statements like that, and I'm in college. And I was—

Where did you go to school?

UC San Diego. [laugh] Me and two hundred other Black people.

Yes, yes. Yes.

Literally. In a school of eighteen thousand undergraduates. I was doing work around reproductive justice and had been for many years at that point. So I entered into that work really through the lens of Planned Parenthood. You know? And I remember sitting in a class. It was a class on human sexuality. And one day they showed us this documentary about Margaret Sanger. Now mind you, I had been organizing a student group called VOX—which is Latin for "voice"—that was like a splinter of Planned Parenthood. It was their campus organizing program. And Planned Parenthood celebrates Margaret Sanger Day. And it's a big deal. Right?

And so here I am in this class, and I'm watching this documentary about Margaret Sanger. And I'm thinking, "She's a racist." Women's lives are complicated because of the ways that we have to navigate patriarchy. She had this vision for women to have access to choice basically about how and when and where you wanted to start a family. And she marries this man, who was actively a part of the eugenics movement and rich. And basically gets him to fund the development of the birth control pill. But then she gets involved in this movement. And these two things start to align where, well, the reason that we need this isn't just about individual choice and self-determination, it's actually about population control and controlling "undesirable" and "deplorable" people, essentially.

I think that's the language they used at that time. And then at the same time, she is also under attack by the state, you know, under these weird Comstock laws [laugh], you know. She's being shaped by and shaping both—from a very reactionary place. Right? And it was actually at that point that I start to feel that I can't work with this group. I had a friend also at the time who was mixed. She was Filipina and white. And she had gone to the Philippines to do this documentary about choice. And she visited a clinic somewhere in the Philippines that Planned Parenthood was operating. She was like, "This shit is so fucked up because they don't have any consideration at all for cultural traditions, beliefs, et cetera." There's this way in which this worldview around choice gets imposed on folks and is used to shame and control their ability to determine whether or not, and when, and how they want to have and be in a family. And so that's how I get introduced to Black feminism because I'm getting introduced in the worst ways to white feminism. [laugh] You know what I mean?

Wrong?

Yeah. It's almost like I would think of white feminism as the less[er] of two evils kind of an approach. And Black feminism was so much more expansive. Like Black feminism, one, acknowledged the humanity of Black people. Right? It starts there. It starts with We are full human beings that deserve to have a choice about how we're in the world. . . . Right?

Who did you read?

Okay. So the first people that I read—the way I got introduced to Combahee actually, if I'm not mistaken, was through *This Bridge Called My Back*, that anthology. And then from there, I started reading all the contributors. I'm like, "Who the fuck are these people?" So then I'm into Barbara Smith. And I get introduced to Audre Lorde around the same time. And I read *Zami*, which changes my entire existence. And then, let me see, actually, I can tell you by looking at my—[looks across bookshelf] a lot of these books I read for classes. Uh-huh, yeah, there's Barbara.

How did *Zami* change your life?

Because it was the first time that I've ever read anything by a Black woman talking in a positive way about being queer and about the contours of queer identity because being queer was also situated very much within whiteness. (There's something up there. There's *Zami* right there.) At the same time, I remember I also took this class about Black nationalism. That's where you get this Rod Bush stuff.

Anyhow, bell hooks, Patricia Hill Collins. My whole worldview changed. Now mind you, here I am also on a campus that is very white and Asian. And we were organizing as students of color around access and retention and climate. And we organized a women of color conference, which actually came before the EWOCC (Empowering Women of Color Conference) E Walk— the one that UC Berkeley does every year . . .

What year is this you're talking about?

I graduated in 2002. So it must have been the year I graduated. I think what I also start to understand more clearly through Black feminism is the ways in which the experiences of Black folks are so layered. And I'm deep in this because I'm a sociology and anthropology major. And of course I'm trying to tease apart all these different things because some of these frameworks are actually very radical and others are not. And depending on who the professor was, they're either laying it out or they're not. [laugh] So it's like this weird schizophrenia almost. But that wasn't unlike my experience in college in this really white-ass place where there's two hundred Black people. And it's a social campus. So we've got our crew of students of color who are organizing. From the standpoint of being students of color and then within that organizing there's lots of conversation about these different ideas and how they apply to our lives and where they don't. There's also this thing that we're bumping up against, which I think is really a product of our time, which is the kind of remnants of multiculturalism and the way in which individual histories get erased because they become a part of this melting pot thing—

Right.

Right? So you're not Black. You're a student of color. [laugh]

Anyhow, organizing in a space that is seen to be predominantly about women—it's very reductionist, but that was kind of the container that it was in at that time—and then also coming into my own identity as a queer Black woman, and then also being in this kind of multicultural organizing space [with] students of color in this campus that is huge. Right? It was being in an oppositional position all the time. Our organizing was oppositional. It was against the administration. And it was against the, like, pervasiveness of whiteness. [laugh] And the fight to actually have space. What appealed to me about Black feminism was it asserted that we deserve space. We deserve space. If you're not dealing with these issues that we have on our backs all the time, you're not getting free, period, dot. We're not even having a conversation until we can start there. So that's my history with it.

Growing up I had this poster in my house from Ntozake Shange's play [*For Colored Girls* . . .]. I was fascinated by it because the woman in that poster looks exactly like my mother. And so I would always say to her, "Mom, is that you?" And she'd be like, "No." I'd be like, "What's it about?" She's like, "It's from this play." But she never talked about it.

Interesting.

It's so strange.

Did all the Black women get that poster?

Maybe. Yeah, so there's that. Part of my time growing up my mother was single. My mom is literally a superhero. You know? She made my clothes because we didn't fucking have money. So she made me clothes that were reversible. [laugh] Which is so brilliant.

I was like, "How did you fucking think of that?" I used to go with her to the fabric store and pick out patterns and stuff. It was really fun. And I was none the wiser. I would say, "This is so cool. I want this one and this one." And she's like, "Great." She knew how to sew, so she made them all. But my mom worked like a million jobs. My uncle, her twin, he helped raised me. And when she met my dad, her circumstances changed somewhat but not really. So she marries this white Jewish man, who has been in my life since I was four. And this is where you start to see a real lack of feminism. So I always had a real—

Can you say more about that? What do you mean?

Well, she is the product of a time when your duties as a wife were to take care of your house and take care of your husband and take care of your children. And all of those things before you do anything for yourself. So my mom is that person who wouldn't eat until everybody else had eaten, even if she had been cooking for eight hours. You know what I mean? My mom is that person who if you wanted something on her plate, she would just give it to you. It didn't matter if she was hungry or not. She's like that to this day, and she's in her sixties. I was not like that. [laugh] And with my dad, you know, we laugh about this now . . . But at the time, it really upset me, and I didn't have language for it until I was exposed to people who put it in words.

My parents had a weird way—I thought it was weird—of interacting. My dad, whom I perceived as laying around, chilling, would be like, "Go get me whatever." And my mom would be like, "Okay." And then when I got old enough, it would be like, "Go get your dad a . . ." And I'd be like, "What the fuck?" We're both sitting here watching TV. You know what I'm saying? I want to watch TV. Why he can't get up and get it himself? Like we're just chilling. And that would get me in a lot of trouble. I realized early on that it wasn't just because I was a child, but also because I was a girl child. My brother never got asked to do any of that shit. He's eight years younger than me. Up until two, three years ago, he still lived with my parents. He doesn't know how to do laundry. He doesn't know how to cook. And I was vacuuming lines into the carpet when I was seven. You know what I'm saying? I could tuck a corner in a bed. [laugh]

My relationship with my dad was very tense for a long time because of that dynamic of patriarchy. And it was certainly also racialized, but in a very weird way for a lot of reasons. But definitely, at the center of it was this idea that you're supposed to do shit for me. You're supposed to make my life easier, and I don't really care what happens. I don't know who makes your life easier, but you're supposed to make my life easier. And then as I was getting older, there was this way that my mom would talk to me about being independent and how important being independent was. And I would try to understand that, since I didn't see her as independent. I was like, yeah, obviously this is really important. I want to do what I want to do, when I want to do it. And I want to be with somebody who wants that for me too. But if you're telling me it's so important, how come you don't have it? And later, as I got older, I came to realize in some ways that is what she wants. Right? So I shouldn't judge, like *you're not independent*. It's more that's what works for her. But it never worked for me. And so having the language to be able to talk about why I deserved to shape my own desires for myself and my life and what I wanted to do, and why it should be possible for me to do it is really important to me. And I feel like I got that a lot from people like bell hooks. You know, recognizing (chuckles) all the ways in which Black women's bodies are objectified, all of the ways in which Black women are stereotyped as overly aggressive. Really, could it be that we're asserting our fucking dignity? You know what I'm saying? And then also ways in which Black women never actually had access to protection as women in the same ways that white women continue to have—all really shaped my experiences.

So in moving forward, in the work that I did and as I learned how to organize, came back to the Bay, and organized in East and West Oakland, all the people I knew who were organizing this—

Organize? What were you doing?

Racial justice, economic justice organizing. So the first thing I started doing was tenant rights organizing in West Oakland. And it was before, it was right when Jerry Brown announced his 10K Plan.* [laughs] And I remember, the summer I started organizing there, we were building toward a community meeting. We were trying to have a hundred new members at a community meeting to talk about Jerry Brown's 10K Plan. So I'm knocking on doors every fucking day during the summer, trying to talk to people, trying to get people to come and get involved. And everyone I knew who was learning how to organize, we had a class of folks, all but three were women.

Right.

---

*The 10K Plan was an urban planning doctrine for Downtown Oakland to attract ten thousand new residents to the city's downtown and Jack London Square areas.

Okay? But in interactions, in community spaces, we were always having to navigate being women outside of the home in a geographical space that is actually held by men, if that makes sense.

And then to get into the house is to be able to have a different kind of interaction with Black women. And that's not necessarily through the, whatever, family structure, but it was just layers. Like to get to a door, you got to cross the street, and there's guys on the street. Right?

Right.

And you have to navigate that as a terrain. And then when you knock on a door, typically, inside the house were Black women. Right? So navigating that. And most of the people we were able to recruit were Black women. Most of the people who were active were Black women. And interestingly, most, if not all, of the organizations that I knew or [was] in relationship to were not led by Black women. They were often led by white folks. So that was a whole thing. And that continued for a while actually.

Across different organizations and organizing projects?

Yeah. The organization I spent the longest time at, ten years almost, was headed by a Black man, and that's why I decided to go there. Because I was like I can't do it any longer. I can't have white supervisors anymore. It's too much. I'm being micromanaged. It mattered to me that I was hired to build a Black organization. And it was really interesting because where I was having to navigate Black feminism, especially organizing in Black communities, was male-dominated spaces, even though Black women were always doing the fucking work. Always. Do you know what I'm saying?

Right.

We ran a campaign for five years that was targeting a developer that was just evil. I mean, like legit evil. They had been the master developer redeveloping the largest remaining Black community left in the city, which is now less than 4 percent Black, down from 13 percent.

What, in Oakland?

San Francisco. Oakland's Black population has dropped significantly, too. We were in this coalition with the Nation of Islam, local preachers, and a couple other local advocates from different groups, environmental groups. And I was often the only woman in the space. So navigating what it meant to, one, not be taken seriously, two, be in a space where power was being exercised, and three, at a certain point in that campaign, I was anointed with more power, but it actually alienated me from other women. It was very interesting. And so, for example, we would have meetings in the mosque. And [laugh] men would sit on one side, and the women would sit on the other. And I—

Really? In a political meeting?

Totally.

Wow.

I would sit wherever the fuck I wanted.

That's absurd.

Right? So then I would sometimes end up sitting on the side with the men mostly because I was like I have to carve out my space. And then that was—

Wow.

Weird. And then being queer was a whole thing. What's the phrase for it? Don't ask, don't tell. [laugh] You know? That's just Alicia, she's interesting. You know what I mean? [laugh] Anyways, all that to say, there's these folks who should go down in history as theorists because they are and theory is not reserved for white people. [laugh] Or for men.

Or for men?

Black feminists' theory was very much based on their own experience having to navigate a world that did not want them. And I think for me Combahee and their work was my cushion and a balm to soothe dynamics that were so troubling and didn't feel like they were going away. You know what I'm saying?

This is really interesting context for the development of the Black Lives Matter network and what has always seemed to be a particular emphasis on Black women leading the organization, and the queer politics that are important in and of themselves but certainly at the center of the organizing as well. Can you say something about what, given those experiences, it means to be not just a women-led organization but for the movement itself, I mean, one of the important characteristics of the movement is that it really is led by women. In some ways, you could say that perhaps for the first time we have a Black social movement that is women-led.

When I met Patrisse [Khan-Cullors] in 2005—

So you guys go way back?

Way back. When I met Patrisse in 2005, she was in Los Angeles at the Labor Community Strategy Center (LCSC). And I was at POWER (People Organized to Win Employment Rights). And our organizations were in relationship to each other. And she and I met at an organizing exchange with nine other groups. It's also how I . . . know most left folks. [laugh] Folks were in coordination and communication around a lot of different things. And so she and I kind of came up together. We're not the same age. I think I'm a little older than she is. But we come into this work at similar times and on the left flank of this work, and shared a lot about what it meant to navigate patriarchy in movement spaces. We talked a lot about this formation that came to be in 2007, and it was a Black left formation. It was groups from across the spectrum, but it was mostly groups rooted in revolutionary nationalism, some kind of grounded in Marxism-Leninism. But whatever the fucking thread was, it was like the practice was so bizarre. Right? At this point I had been with POWER for a couple years. And I got invited to attend this political meeting with the director of the organization. And I remember walking into this room, and it was all men, every last person, except for maybe two—and I mean, of all ages.

What was going on?

It was crazy. And it was me. I think Patrisse was there. I think she was there. It was me, her, and two older sisters, one of whom I knew, and the other whom I didn't. And that was it. And there were 150 people in this room. And I feel a way, right, when people who are not Black talk about how patriarchal Black people are. I feel weird about that. But then being in it, I'm like, no, we have some work to do. You know what I'm saying?

So here we are in this meeting. And this brother talked for a good thirty minutes. And when he was done, I remember I raised my hand. And I said, "I really appreciate most of what you said. But the question that I'm trying to answer is where do I fit in any of this because you have not talked about Black women. You have not talked about Black queer folks. You have not talked about Black trans folks. And how that fits into your vision of liberation. I'm a Black queer woman. And I'm not just organizing Black people so other people can get free. I want to get free. So based on your framework, how do I get down? I want to be a part of this team. I want to build Black liberation. So where do I fit?" And the room—silent. It was silent for a good twenty seconds, and people are looking at each other. [laugh] And I'm there with my boss. And so I'm like, "Did I say something wrong? Did I miss something?" You know what I'm saying? And then they just moved on. Legit, moved on.

Wow.

Like, "Next question." Silence. Patrisse tells the story about how she asked a similar question at one of these same meetings. And somebody got so fucking mad at her, they spit in her fucking face. And they said some shit like, "We're not down with the gay agenda." Or something. And this was in the year 2006. I mean, how sway?! You know what I'm saying? Meanwhile, we don't have infrastructure to leave anybody behind.

It'd be one thing if we were strong as fuck, right, and just winning all this shit. And then people come with *what about me?* I could see a perspective that would be like, "What about you? We have everything we need." You know what I'm saying? You're going to get in line or you're not. But it's like we don't have any of those things. [laugh] And yet still you're throwing people away.

Right? And there were queer Black folks that I would talk to that I would process the stuff with. And they'd be like, "I don't think they're homophobic." I'd be like, "No, no, I'm sure they're nice people, but that's not what I'm talking about." I can't continue to be a part of this group that is not thinking about anybody else but Black men. I'm not interested in that. So there's that. And I'm tired of having to be smart enough to jab with people just to get my fucking point across, which is that we need to be at the center of this vision. [laugh] Do you know what I'm saying? And the ways in which, you know how people on the left can be. It's like we just dissect shit to death. You know, and that's not the right line and blah, blah, blah. And I'm like, "Okay. All that's fine. But what about the folks that we're actually accountable to? What about people like your wife or your daughter? Don't you want something more for them?" Do you know what I'm saying? Like even if whatever you think for yourself, don't you want freedom for your family, for your loved ones?

Did you ask that?

Well, I didn't, and I'll tell you why. Because I came to realize that with a lot of those folks they didn't have the most loving relationships with their partners and daughters. Do you know what I'm saying? And so, you know, this isn't going to be a secret to you, but some of the sharpest, most visionary, most revolutionary men were beating their wives, were abusive to them. So, of course not. I mean, if you can exist in a space where your wife can't be then you're clearly not tripping about . . . [laugh] You know what I'm saying? If you could look around a room and be like, "Why is my life partner not here?" and feel okay with that, then you're really not worried about the future.

So how does that shape your—

So I was giving that context to ground where and how those ideas get infused into Black Lives Matter, because it was actually really intentional. And a lot of it had to do with experiences like that, that Patrisse and I had both had, and really wanting to have political space where we could be all of who we were and not be seen as weird or some anomaly and also not be taken less seriously. And when [George] Zimmerman was acquitted, and I popped off on Facebook, said some shit, and then Patrisse was like, "We need to make this a thing." We thought, okay. Well, if we're going to build a political project, which was how we envisioned Black Lives Matter before all this, everything that this is now. We talked about, well, what is the framework? Right? And the way that we actually got a lot clearer about it was when we started this, the response pushed us to be clearer about what we meant. We created a space to talk about state-sanctioned violence and anti-Black racism. It started for us with Trayvon [Martin]. But then we started to see how there were these tropes and also ways that we were playing into it too. So our early logo was actually an image of a Black man in a hoodie.

I didn't know that.

Right? And now when I'm looking at it, I'm like, "Shit. Why did we choose that?" So we started to see that the conversations that were happening were conversations that were like save the Black man, and our Black boys are being murdered in the streets. You know what I mean? And then meanwhile it was Black women doing this work.

I'll try to tell this story in a short way, but it's helpful to understand how this came to be so clearly this political. There's a gallery downtown——I won't go into names and stuff. But we actually had a very intentional conversation. And they hit me up one time. Somebody who I have known for a really long time, white dude, who is chill, has been in the movement for a long time. They were doing an art show at their space. And they wanted to center it around Black people who had been killed by the police. They asked us to send some materials. And it kind of irritated me. When I got their request I was like, "Materials?" Like why the fuck wouldn't you ask me to help you shape it? You just told me we're basing this off the work that you've done. "So can you send us some materials?" Well, who's participating in it? Who have you been talking to? Right? So they're like, "Well, we're talking to Color of Change. And we picked these artists." Oh, man. So one of the brothers was an indigenous brother, who is super chill. And he had done this series called *Justice for Our Lives*, this brother Oree, who is really dope. Another person, Ajuan, who is a Black, masculine-of-center woman, who does this series called *1001 Black Men*. I was like, "Damn, you're really going to . . .?" And she literally has done a thousand and one or more portraits of Black men specifically. And then this other brother, who——I can't remember his name. I've probably blocked it out because he really pissed me off.

[laugh]

His work was in there. I had a feeling about it, but I was like maybe I'm just being sensitive. Because this was right around the time that people started to do this fucking weird All Lives Matter, Brown Lives Matter, Black and Brown Lives Matter thing. So I was deep in the thick of "Why are people doing that?" And being here in the Bay where I've organized for a long time, I was really struggling with my own political community around why it was okay just to talk about Black people. I know that your shit is fucked up too, but can we just talk about Black people? And it was a real struggle. So I thought that's why I was having some feelings. A couple days after we had this interaction, I read this article on Facebook that's an interview with one of these artists, and he's talking about how he basically came up with Black Lives Matter. This is how they wrote the article. Right? So this artist is the leading edge of Black Lives Matter. And I was like, "What in the fuck." And it was in an artist magazine, but it was getting traction on Facebook. And I was really fucking pissed.

Wow.

I was like, ain't this some shit. Like first of all—because actually before he called it Justice for Our Lives, it was called Black Lives Matter. And they asked him, "How did you start this?" And he was like, "Oh, I started it after like Oscar Grant," or some shit. And I was like, "What in the entire fuck." Like, hello, you know. And so I lost my shit, and I called Patrisse. And I was pissed. I mean, I was pacing. I remember I was at the bar. And I was out front, pacing. I was on the phone, and I was smoking. I'm like, "And then these motherfuckers," you know what I mean, literally going wild. And she's like, "Yo, you need to write, yo, because you're tripping right now."

This is where the herstory came from.

Yes. And I was like, "I don't have time for it." She's like, "Dude, you need to write. You need to write this down. People need to hear why it's not okay. And then we figure out what we're going to do with these folks because that's not okay." So I sat in the corner of my little spot that I love, and I wrote this piece called "Erasing the Black from Black Lives Matter." And the editors at the *Feminist Wire* changed the title to "The Herstory of the Black Lives Matter Movement." But it was all about, right, why it's not okay to take Black queer women's work and legit reappropriate it and then spit it back out like it's your own. And it doesn't have the same content. It doesn't have the same sharpness. It just doesn't have any of what it's supposed to have.

And so I talked about that. I talked about being asked to do labor for this show that was my own fucking work. I'm supposed to [laugh]—you know what I mean? Oh, you just want me to bring materials? Wow, you and a bunch of other people shape a conversation that you haven't fucking been a part of. Where do they do that? And then it's all focused on men. So like Brother Oree, who I love, didn't have no pictures of Black women killed, Black queer people killed. So it was just men.

And then they also still did that thing where it was like Black and Brown, all lives. So they called the show "Justice for Our Lives," and I was pissed. I was pissed. I was like, no, no, no, no. So that's where that came from. I actually was in conversation with my homegirl, who is Chicana. She's actually Chicana and Japanese. And I was like talking to her. And I was like, "Am I missing something? Where does the piece about how we're not in solidarity come in if I'm talking about how Black people are specifically impacted?" She was like, "No, not only do I feel you, I actually feel like the conversation needs to be put back to Brown folks around anti-Blackness because we're anti-Black as fuck." Right? And I was like, "Wow." So there was that whole thing. And then talking to my friend Merv, who is Afro–Puerto Rican. I was talking to Merv about it, too, and being like, "How can we talk about the layered experiences that Black folks have? And what is the impact on us when we assume that 'Black' means one thing?" Like people be like, "Well, what about immigrants?" It's like, "Black people are immigrants." You know what I'm saying? Black people are everything. And so, yeah, all that was happening, so that was like a collectively shaped piece. And then we actually had a dialogue with the artists and the gallery owner that was facilitated by a Black woman to talk about this is why this is not okay. And we're not trying to punish you. We want you to—if I took your One Hundred Black Men series and took your fucking name off it, changed the background colors, and tried to repackage it, that's how we feel right now.

And turn it into One Hundred White Babies. [laugh]

Like you feel a way. Right? So we had a whole conversation. It was really interesting because the Black man would not show up to the conversation.

Really?

He would not show up to the conversation. He was like, "I'm offended. I'm offended that these questions are even being asked. You don't know my work. You don't know this." And it was like it's not about any of that. So he didn't even participate. Oree and Ajuan did. And it was really a good conversation that shifted some stuff I think. We could get into all that. But that's where that comes from. It was like we're not going to fucking be erased again. I'm not going to argue with you about where this started. [laugh] You know what I mean? And I'm going to fight for my shit. And if we're going to change the way that we organize, we have to stop doing this. Like this framework of multiracial organizing is so sloppy because it allows us to not take responsibility for the ways that we also perpetuate systems. Like anti-Blackness is the fulcrum around which white supremacy works. Right? And so it's not that Brown folks are not impacted. It's not that. People are going back and forth like, "Well, Latinos are killed more," da-da-da. And I was like, "Well, there's fucking more of you all numerically than Black people." Right? [laugh] I mean, if we're going to do like statistics like that, let's talk about in relationship to population. It's fucked up that all people are getting killed. We're getting killed *disproportionately*, and we should be thinking about rather than competing, we should be thinking about how we can talk about the different ways that we're targeted because we're not targeted in the same way. And inasmuch as they're related, the idea of who is a criminal is based on Black bodies. And so sorry that you have joined the club. [laugh] You know what I'm saying? But we have to be able to get into that. And when we always approach this question from a perspective of Black and Brown, we're actually erasing people in that. Right? Like Black people are also Latinos. Latino does not mean Brown. It does not mean the absence of Black. Right? And in that conversation we're still erasing Black folks, which is hella anti-Black. Right? So lots of that.

Let me just ask you about that. How has it shaped the network nationally or here locally, the ability to work in coalition or develop solidarity between groups that are impacted by state violence? How do those things work together?

Well, I think that those early interventions actually created space for new work to happen. So one person I think it would be awesome if you wanted to talk with is my sister Marisa Franco, who is coordinating this network called Mijente. And I suggest her because their whole network was built in this context where she felt Latinos need to get in line and on board. Right? We're fighting this fight around immigration reform, which is quickly turning into a fight around criminalization, and nobody wants to talk about that. Right?

Right. Yeah.

And they've actually done some really interesting work, but they also came out pretty hard after Mike Brown was killed. And they were one of the only non-Black, Latino-led groups that were like, "Not only are we taking leadership from Black folks, but we want to talk about anti-Blackness in our own communities and how some of our people are supporting people like George Zimmerman, or supporting people like Darren Wilson, because of the way in which criminal behavior is defined and because of the way in which Black bodies are criminalized." So that's an example of I think how folks have been shaped by this movement, Black folks and other folks of color. But I would say the Bay is a specific place. And it has its own history, patterns, traditions, like every other place. But it also has way more infrastructure than many places throughout the country. So what the Bay looked like, we didn't actually start a chapter here until 2014.

And we did it really slowly mostly because we were like, "Is that our best contribution to this movement?" We have everything here. You know what I mean? But what we didn't have was a space for Black organizers. Every Black organizer that I knew was organizing in a multiracial organization in which Black people were severely underrepresented. So it was like we're a Black and Brown organization, but you are actually a Latino organization with Black members. [laugh] You know what I'm saying? And it's all good, but that's what it is. So there's that. I think one way that it helped to shape this particular landscape was that Black folk actually came together. And our chapter is almost like an umbrella of different organizations and Black leadership from inside those organizations. You know? It transformed people's organizations because folk were like, "Well, now the Black people are doing some shit together."

[laugh] What are we doing in this organization to be responsive to this moment?

I think what I know about that call is that it is one that lots of people reference in how they came into this moment. And as you know, there's lots of tension among folk who, you know, about the ways in which attention has been taken from places like Ferguson or Baltimore. I think they rest blame in the wrong place, but I understand the dynamic that they're talking about. It's not new. Even happened after Hurricane Katrina. That's the left. [laugh] It's not BLM. And it's also America and how short our attention spans are and all of that. But a lot of people that I talk to say that they have read that letter, and that is the basis upon which they have built their work. So when it comes to shaping, well, what do we believe, they use that. They use our guiding principles, which really affirms the dignity and humanity of all Black people. And I think we're now at a point where we're realizing it was an important catalyst, and it's not enough. Right? Now there's some stuff for us to get into around power and influence. And what does it mean to transform the way that power operates in this country? What does that mean for Black people? How do we not perpetuate the same systems of domination inside of our own work or as we reimagine what our communities can look like and what our institutions can and should look like? How are we deep enough in that politics to not do the thing where it's like I don't care about anything else but Black folks?

Or the thing where it's like, well, no other people of color have shown up for me so I'm not showing up for them, which is not fucking true. And that's also why Combahee and all these other writings are really important because back in the day folk were talking about themselves as "third-world women," which I think is a way better unifier than "women of color."

But that's a solidarity term and not a political identity, and I think people miss that. There's also not a lot of places where people are being trained politically, except in the academy. And the academy is not sufficient to train people politically I think, especially when it comes to what it means to build power with people who have a wide spectrum of ideas, experience, and relationship to power. You know?

Yes.

That has to be our next phase. And in a Trump era where Blackness will be reconnected to this idea of law and order, and where Black people, some Black people will come out [of] the woodwork, saying I like this new deal for Black America because finally somebody is paying attention to us. It is a different phenomenon than under Obama, but it will be equally as painful. Our task right now is to think about what movement building can look like from a perspective of making sure that our movement is not anti-Black and making sure that that doesn't mean Black dogmatism.

The chapters that are the most developed are ones that have taken that theory and put it into practice and then reshaped the theory to help understand what it means for us then to be organizing in a place like Chicago, where people are dying every day. And this narrative of criminality is being attached as an inherent trait of Black people as opposed to a condition, like a symptom of systems. And they're grappling with how we interact with power. They don't meet with police, for example, because they're like, we don't see the police on the side of social change so we don't have anything to negotiate about. [laugh] Right? Places like Minneapolis, where folks occupied for forty-something days and got shot at and wounded by white supremacists. Avowed white supremacists who got on social media and talked about what the fuck they were going to do and then did it. You know what I'm saying? Those are the chapters that have built a base and are thinking about knowing that it takes protest and more to change the systems and the structures that impact our lives.

And so if I could go back and add to that piece, I would add something about power. I would add something about how our movements can't only be composed of the people who are most disenfranchised. Our movements also have to be composed of people from across the class spectrum and people who also have power. Right? If we want to compete for power, then part of what it means is we have to amass our power as a unit. And it also means we have to take some of theirs. That's how you compete, right? You've got to break some of their folks off and be like, "Well, which side are you actually on?" Right? And it also means that our vision for what a new society can look like has to appeal to more than just the intellectual class of activists and organizers.

So I think what we are grappling with at this time and what Combahee makes me think about now is that that was such a powerful statement of unity and clarity about what brings us together, even though we don't all live the same life. That's the next step our movement has to take. What brings us together even though we don't all share the same life? We share the same aspirations. We yearn for the same things. And so what does it mean for us then to be in deep and principled relationship with each other? And to be not just wanting to be at the table—I love me some Solange—but we don't just want a seat at the table.

We want the table. And we want to decide who is sitting at the table.

Right.

[laugh] Right? And then maybe we want to get rid of the table.

Well, that's actually my last question, which is—

You didn't know I was a talker, did you? [laugh]

No, no, no, it's great. Part of the core politics, it seems to me, of Black feminism is anticapitalism; that ran through.

Yeah. Yeah.

I mean, there's part of the tensions with white feminism.

[laugh] Because they're ambivalent about capitalism.

Right. And so I'm wondering if those politics also shape your view of things, like where the movement needs to go. Is that something that you think is agreed upon or even understood within the movement? Is that controversial? What is the—how do people view anticapitalism or even socialism? Because those two things aren't necessarily the same thing. But when we talk about alternatives to what currently exists, what are those conversations about?

I think, to be honest with you, from my vantage point, I think those conversations are still in process. I think that there's lots of folks who move from a position of anticapitalism who wouldn't name themselves anticapitalist, and mostly because there are certain frameworks that are associated with the white left, even though our people have a rich, rich history. I mean, fucking you go back to at least the thirties.

Yes.

But it's one of the challenges of our moment. Let me just use this example. And then I'll answer the question more directly. When I was in school, which is the first place that I got intentionally exposed to political work, I took a sociology class on Marx and didn't come out politicized in any kind of way because it was being taught in a very apolitical way. [laugh] And I was very resistant to it until I started to understand frameworks of anticapitalism within, through a Black lens. So a friend of mine was like, "We just started a study group on Black Marxism." I was like, "I got to get back into that." I tried it. We got about a hundred pages in and I was like, I don't understand what he's talking about. [laugh]

[laugh]

God bless his soul. So I'll say this, I think there are some of us who are socialists. I think there are some of us who are anticapitalist. There's not enough of us who are anti-imperialist, which I actually feel like is really needed. And I think that what this moment calls for is a real investment in studying models. When I was watching some of the commentary around Fidel, I was like, "COINTEL-PRO fucked our shit up." You know?

What do you mean?

Well, what I mean is the impact and influence of COINTELPRO decimated the infrastructure that we needed to train people politically and to grapple with the question of alternatives, which are villainized here. Fidel Castro is a polarizing figure to people who are really invested in capitalism. And as I [was] watching all the back and forth between people who would be like, "You're not from Cuba. You don't know," and da-da-da. And I was like, I just don't even think that's it. That's the kind of politics that's not going to get us anywhere. And Black folks do it too: "If you're not Black, you can't tell me." And it's like, "Well, I'm not sure that's true." I think what we're trying to offer is that when you attempt to dismantle a global system and a global organizing principle, there are all kinds of ways in which the state tries to discourage that.

Absolutely.

And it has a lot to do also with like demonizing places and people that are trying new shit. I mean, people did the same shit with Chávez while he was alive—and certainly after his death. And now look at the fucking state of Venezuela. Right? Even Martin [King], you know, as Martin was starting to become more explicitly anticapitalist, though I would say he was probably anti-interventionist–anti-imperialist before he was anticapitalist, but that's when he was assassinated. Like, yeah, I don't think so. So in terms of where I feel like our movement is going, we're starting to figure out what's the new Black lens that we are going to see ever-changing systems through. What is capitalism right now? Are we in a moment where neoliberal capitalism is on the decline and some other kind of capitalism is on the rise? We don't know. We don't know what capitalism under Trump is going to look like. But neoliberalism is not going to be—I don't think that it's going to be the central organizing principle for this next period. And then you have people that would be like, "I'm an anarchist." You know? But one of the things that I think really is a loss for our generation is that the vision for alternatives is not driven and led by Black folk.

Let me just give you another quick example. I was in a conversation with someone about Standing Rock. And they were going crazy because they were like, "It's not a victory, and none of this matters." I'm like, "It's totally a victory, *and* they're going to keep drilling." They're going to keep drilling. It is still a victory that you got Obama's lame ass to step in. You know?

Yes.

You didn't fix anything. You just changed the balance of forces, that's all. And that's a big deal. And you should celebrate that because people put work into that shit. It's seventeen degrees, and there are seven thousand people out there. Let's be clear. This person's whole thing was, "Well, people are going to think it's a victory so they're going to leave." And I was said, "Well, I trust the organizers, and I don't think that's going to happen. And frankly, you're on the wrong thread. I know it's not a victory in the way that you're talking about it. It's not the end. But it's a victory. It's a step."

There are no victories until the final barricade [laugh] has been overturned.

Of course. And then the person said, "It's going to make all the white people leave." And I was like, "Well, I really hope your strategy wasn't predicated on white people because they just cannot be depended on yet, not in that way." [laugh] You know what I'm saying? Please, god, tell me that's not what your strategy is based on. Because, yes, white people will leave you. That is what they do. You know what I'm saying? That's historical. Please tell me your strategy is not built there. I tell this story to say that they said, "Well, I've been telling people not to close their Wells Fargo accounts. That instead, they should run up the bill and then not pay it and make Wells Fargo pay . . ." And I was like, "That's so interesting because white people get to do that shit. What about people's credit? What are you talking about? Just run your thing and don't pay the bill? Who the fuck?" You know what I'm saying?

White people think that way because you don't have consequences. And that's the thing, when we're reimagining an economy and a democracy, if it's led by white people, we will fucking get left behind. My nervousness right now is around the alternatives that are being put forward by non-alternative leaders—I said it: an absence of identity politics, and it's a gentle capitalism, which will not be gentle on Black people. It will be softer on the white middle class. I mean, they're very explicit about that. They're like, "We want to make capitalism better for the middle strata. [laugh] And we'd prefer it if it was the white middle strata."

I'm in a weird place where, for my cohort, our parents and our peers had and have different options under an expanding, less liberal democracy. The cohort that comes up after me doesn't have that. They're post attacks on the public sector. So we also have different political visions about what's possible, which is why we also have different political reads about what time it is. For some folk, they're like, "I'm just fucked." And it doesn't feel any different to me. I don't agree with it. I see it differently because I also have a different experience that's on my back. They don't. So I appreciate that. But, I think just like we have Black feminism, we need a new vision for Black socialism. We need a new vision for Black power that doesn't throw anyone away, and that doesn't replicate the same shit that we have right now, which is not working for us, even when we think it does.

Well, it's working for some people.

Very few. It's like Oprah and Samuel L. Jackson. Right?

And those thirteen thousand elected officials. But, yeah.

It's dwindling every day. So what's exciting for me is I think that part of why we established this frame as not just being about police violence was to be able to take in and take on the totality of the state apparatus. And police are like the tip of the iceberg. They're the most visible part of the state.

Right.

So this, to me, feels like a moment where people are being compelled to understand the state in a different way, as we develop our strategies for building power and hopefully ultimately for taking power. And the thing that I'm hoping happens too in this movement is a different way of relating to electoral organizing because that's where decisions are being made. And beyond that, when I think about Cuba, when I think about any successful political revolution, they had to demonstrate that they could govern. And I think that's why our track record is not so good. You know? We don't know what it looks like to run cities in ways that actually improve Black people's lives. We know what it looks like to have a Black city council and a Black mayor and have it be corrupt as fuck. [laugh] Do you know what I'm saying?

We know that too well.

Yeah. So we have some uphill battles to take on.

But do you think that's possible—to learn how to govern in this context?

I think we have to. Even if it's at the smallest level. Do you know what I'm saying?

Yeah.

Like Black people need to run the transit board. Black people need to run the water board. Black people need to run the school board. Those are sites of shaping. And when you can tangibly say, "This is how I've improved your life," it allows for people to break with what they don't love but they don't know anything else. And I think we're in that place where we can talk as much shit about how fucked up things are, but when folks don't know anything else they either don't participate or they make the wrong choice because it's safer than not knowing. You know?

So that's what I think about it. And I think on the movement level, it's hard to say. It's too early to say where people are going to end up. But what I'm hearing people talk about is independent political power for Black folks. And when I think about political power I can't separate it from electoral organizing. I do separate it from Democrats and Republicans. Electoral organizing is still a vehicle that most people participate in. And if it wasn't important for Black folks to be in that, they wouldn't try to take it from us.

COMMENTS BY BARBARA RANSBY

at Socialism 2017 Conference Panel

Fortieth Anniversary of the Combahee River Collective Statement

I was not in the Combahee River Collective, but I was inspired by the Combahee River Collective. As a historian, I want to preface my remarks with a few critical comments and observations. One is that sometimes we talk about these empowering, important historical moments, and we are looking for blueprints or road maps. Unfortunately, history does not offer us that. We have our own work to do, in our own time. Nevertheless, looking at the Combahee River Collective statement and praxis does situate us in a certain trajectory of history that many writers on the left have ignored. It foregrounds and centers the organizing and intellectual work of radical Black feminists who were also lesbians. So it is important to mark that fact.

The other thing I want to do is to pay tribute to the founders of the Combahee River Collective (CRC). They would be the first to tell you that we also cannot romanticize those moments. CRC founders have talked about the good times, but within every strug-

gle that we look back upon with rose-colored glasses, there was another layer of struggle, right? There were the struggles within the
struggle. And they persevered. So I think those are important les-
sons and caveats. The third thing is something that Barbara Smith
has alluded to, which is that there is a kind of artificial way that
we try to tame the timelines of the past. We put them in brackets
of periods and so forth. Historians are trained to do that. But, in
fact, the Combahee River Collective was embedded in a specific
period of struggle defined by a number of significant events and
thrusts. For example, 2017 is also the fiftieth anniversary of the
1967 Detroit rebellion, which had a powerful impact on my own
political consciousness. I grew up in Detroit. I was ten years old
in 1967 when the rebellion occurred. And I see the CRC's work
and the explosion of protest in the summer of 1967 as very much
related. Black feminism didn't grow on another planet and then
drop down on this one. In fact it was a product of, and influenced
by, the larger movements of its time. And in fact, I would say it is
the umbrella under which we have to see that larger Black political
past, beginning in the early 1960s.

Barbara Smith and Demita Frazier have laid out some of the
background and the history of CRC. But I want to say, too, that
the Combahee River Collective Statement, as well as the example
of the Combahee River Collective, laid the ground for a number of
projects that came after that. African American Women in Defense
of Ourselves (AAWIDO) was a project I was very involved in, in
1991. It was an effort by Black feminists to respond to the nomina-
tion of sexist and conservative Clarence Thomas to the US Supreme
Court. We argued that Thomas's use of the language of race—he
charged his critics with engaging in a "high tech lynching"—was
actually a perversion of the struggle against racism and white supremacy, and the public discourse ignored the complex reality of

Black women's lived experiences. As people will recall, Thomas's appointment to the court was almost derailed by credible allegations of sexual harassment by a Black woman attorney and legal scholar, Anita Hill, who previously worked for Thomas. AAWIDOO was a response to the Thomas–Hill controversy that inserted a gender analysis and sharply criticized Thomas. We collected 1,600 names of Black women signatories, raised tens of thousands of dollars (before crowdsourcing or even the Internet) and placed paid full-page ads in major newspapers, including the *New York Times*, in order to ensure our voices were heard. We were emboldened to take that action by the example set by our Combahee sisters.

Moreover, in 1991, after AAWIDOO's ad campaign was launched, Barbara Smith stepped forward and said, "This is a historic moment and struggle. We're going to do a poster." Kitchen Table Press, which she had founded, designed and printed a poster that included the statement that we had written, with red, black, and green border, and listing the sixteen hundred and five names of people who had contributed to that ad. So that was a beautiful moment.

These are examples of continuities but also examples of the moments of struggle where campaigns and organizations intersect. Barbara Smith and I worked together again during the Black Radical Congress [from] 1996 to '98. Black Radical Congress was a major convening here in Chicago that was over two years in the planning. It included two thousand radical Black organizers, scholars, and artists. And as Barbara Smith said at the time, it was the first time that Black feminism was included as a legitimate plank of a larger multifaceted Black radical tradition. In other words, revolutionary nationalists, socialists, and communists were included historically. They all represented very male-centered discourses around revolution and struggle. However, radical Black feminism, in the tradition of the Combahee River Collective, had simply not been included as a part of a Black radical tradition. And in 1998 it was.

The authors of the Combahee River Collective Statement have reminded us over and over again that this was a left document. It was a socialist document. It offered a platform that had enormous depth and breadth. And so this offers us a window into understanding the role of radical Black feminism, which is really a road map for liberation. In many Black feminist circles, CRC statement is seen as sacred text, and I say that as a pretty committed secularist.

The statement and the practice that surrounded it debunks the notion that so-called identity politics represents a narrowing rather than a broadening of our collective political vision. The document is antiracist, anticapitalist, anti-imperialist, and anti-hetero-patriarchy. That is CRC's Black feminist agenda.

There are five critical principles we can draw from the statement. One is that it is materialist. People talk about, where did their politics come from? It came from the lived experiences of Black women: of poor and working-class Black women. Not all Black women, but some of the most oppressed sectors of our communities. So Michelle Obama, Oprah Winfrey, and Beyoncé live a little bit of a different life. They don't embody the common experience of the majority of Black women. So, we can never talk about any group as a monolith.

The other principle that I take away from the work of the CRC is the one of self-determination. They insisted this: "If we don't love ourselves, if we don't work for our own liberation, who will do that?" That is the principle of self-determination. And they were explicitly anticapitalist and pro-socialist: unapologetically so. Here is a direct quote, "We recognize that the liberation of all oppressed people necessitates the destruction of the political-economic systems of capitalism and imperialism, as well as patriarchy." There was no ambivalence, no confusion about where they stood.

The CRC statement embodied intersectionality before "intersectionality" was a coined term. They were dealing with the intimate relationship between the variables of race, class, as well as sex, describing them as "simultaneous factors in our oppression while at the same time rejecting any form of biological determinism." That is a very important and sophisticated concept in terms of how we wage class struggle. Their understanding of the role of patriarchy and white supremacy is clear. Finally, their work embodied radically democratic practices. The last page of the document reads: "We believe in collective process and a nonhierarchical distribution of power within our own group and in our vision of a revolutionary society." That expression was very important. I write about Ella Baker's principles of nonhierarchical leadership. That is embedded and embodied in the Combahee River Collective Statement.

So, CRC is an important legacy. However, the question, where do we look for radical Black feminist leadership today, remains. The Black Lives Matter movement, and Movement for Black Lives, writ large, and inclusive of many organizations and coalitions, is where the contemporary Black freedom movement has landed in many ways. And this movement—not without problems or contradictions, but on the whole—has embraced a radical Black feminist praxis as its ideological bedrock. And that is pivotal to recognize. Because then we see, from the protests in the streets of Hamburg and London, the politics of intersectionality. In the expanded sanctuary and reparations movements, in the Resist Reimagine Rebuild coalition in Chicago, we see the politics of the Combahee River Collective. In the protests of resistance, when the cop who murdered Philando Castile was let off, we see an intersectional analysis. If you listen to the speeches that people are making and the connections that groups like Black Youth Project 100 and others are making between race, class, and state violence, you see a Combahee analysis. BYP100 in particular insists that its work against economic injustice and police violence is being deployed through a "queer Black feminist lens." When you see Black feminist delegations led by groups like Florida's Dream Defenders, we see the internationalism of the Combahee River Collective has carried over to this generation of Black activists.

All of the work going on in the spirit of Combahee has also not been easy. We see a steady and growing backlash against the current Black freedom movement just as the Combahee River Collective experienced this in its own time. People may have seen the recent *Buzzfeed* article that really focused a laser beam attack against the Black feminist leaders of the Black Lives Matter movement. That is not to suggest that people can't be critical or that the movement shouldn't be self-critical. But that article in particular was selective in its harsh and biased attack on the women leaders of the movement. Similarly, in the *New York Times*, about a week ago [June 27, 2017], a response to the pro-Palestinian stance of the Chicago Dyke March completely denigrated the very concept of intersectionality, arguing that it was selective and divisive. The other read of the Dyke March's action—to not allow what they defined as a Zionist flag in the parade—was a group of activists defining solidarity as a matter of principle and not simple identity. They were not simply all women or all lesbians, they were queer women with very specific visions of what justice for all should look like, and that does not include occupation or settler colonialism. The writer, Bari Weiss, in the op-ed page of the *New York Times*, said intersectionality is the problem with the left today. That is an odd assertion to say the least.

What does that assertion even mean? It means all of the lame coalitions that are saying, "Put all of your differences on the back burner. Don't talk about race. Don't talk about gender. Don't talk about sexuality. Just talk about class." This approach led us to a false unity, because we have glossed over who we are and what privileges we enjoy, and oppression we suffer, as a result. The nexus between the power of radical Black feminism and the power of those forces who have the courage to speak out in solidarity with Palestine—together represent threats to a neoliberal frame and worldview. Fortunately, groups like the Jewish Voice for Peace, who stand resolutely with the cause of Palestinian freedom, have offered an alternative view to the dominant one. They have, along with our Palestinian comrades, been very courageous and very outspoken in that regard.

Let me just say three things in closing. If we take to heart the spirit and politics of the Combahee River Collective Statement, what we go away with is this: (1) never be afraid to speak truth to power, and (2) in the face of racist, misogynist threats of violence and attacks, when you have the impulse to either fight or flight, what do you do? Fight! And, (3) always ally yourself with those on the bottom, on the margins, and at the periphery of the centers of power. And in doing so, you will land yourself at the very center of some of the most important struggles of our society and our history.

The final thought I will share is this.

The larger-than-life Cuban revolutionary Che Guevara once said, "Every revolutionary is motivated by great feelings of love." And we have to take from that, never hesitate to love your people, and the people who struggle alongside you, but also never be afraid to critique and struggle with those you love.

ACKNOWLEDGMENTS

It has been a tremendous honor to work on this small book. I want to thank Julie Fain and Anthony Arnove for encouraging me to follow through on what I think is an important project.

All books are collective efforts and this one is no different. I want to thank the wonderful staff at Haymarket for their dedication, professionalism, and commitment to getting the work done. I want to especially thank Dào Tran for her initial comments and queries in an effort to help me shape this book in its earliest stages. I want to also thank Caroline Luft, who played a critical role as an editor. Caroline was interested, observant, smart, and sharp throughout this process, and her contributions have made this book possible.

But the biggest thanks go to the women who helped make this book a possibility because of their enormous generosity in granting me the time and privilege to interview them. So, thanks to Barbara Smith, Demita Frazier, Beverly Smith, and Alicia Garza. Thank you to Barbara Ransby, who allowed me to use her brilliant comments about the Combahee River Collective that she gave at the Socialism 2017 conference in Chicago.

I wish to thank my wife and partner, Lauren Fleer, and our toddler, Ellison, for their enduring patience, love, and solidarity.

Finally, this book is dedicated to my mother, Doris Jeanne

Merritt Taylor. Through the process of making this book I came
to understand more about my mother's all-too-short life. A working-class Black woman from Nashville, Tennessee, she embodied
the "interlocking oppressions" at the heart of the Combahee analysis. As is the case with millions of Black women in this country, the
stresses and strains of that history, overlaid with the responsibilities
of being a single mother, are the toxic brew of premature death. Let
us end the economic system that devours the people we love.

CONTRIBUTOR BIOGRAPHIES

Keeanga-Yamahtta Taylor is author of *From #BlackLivesMatter to Black Liberation,* published by Haymarket Books in January 2016. The book surveys the historical and contemporary ravages of racism and persistent structural inequality, including mass incarceration, housing discrimination, police violence, and unemployment. Taylor is the recipient of the 2016 Cultural Freedom Especially Notable Book Award from the Lannan Foundation.

Taylor's interests are broadly in the fields of race and public policy, Black politics, and racial inequality in the United States. Her writing has been published in *Souls: A Critical Journal of Black Politics, Culture and Society, The Guardian, Los Angeles Times, Boston Review, New Republic, Al Jazeera America, Jacobin, In These Times, New Politics, The International Socialist Review*, and other publications. She is currently writing a book titled *Race for Profit: Black Housing and the Urban Crisis in the 1970s*, under contract with the University of North Carolina Press in their Justice, Power, and Politics series. Taylor received her PhD in African American studies at Northwestern University in 2013 and is currently assistant professor of African American studies at Princeton University.

Barbara Smith is an author, activist, and independent scholar who has played a groundbreaking role in opening up a national dialogue about the intersections of race, class, sexuality, and gender. She is coeditor of *Conditions: Five, The Black Women's Issue* (1979); *All the Women Are White, All the Blacks Are Men, But Some of Us Are Brave: Black Women's Studies* (1982); and *The Reader's Companion to U. S. Women's History* (1998). She is editor of *Home Girls: A Black Feminist Anthology* (1983). Smith coauthored *Yours in Struggle: Three Feminist Perspectives on Anti-Semitism and Racism* (1984). Her essays, *The Truth That Never Hurts: Writings on Race, Gender, and Freedom,* were published in 1998. *Ain't Gonna Let Nobody Turn Me Around: Forty Years of Movement Building with Barbara Smith*, edited by Alethia Jones and Virginia Eubanks, was published in 2014. She was cofounder and publisher of Kitchen Table: Women of Color Press. In 2005 she was elected to the Albany, New York, Common Council and served two terms (2006–2013).

Beverly Smith worked in public and community health in the Boston area after completing her master of public health degree at Yale University. Her commitment to the health and well-being of Black women has been a focus of her professional life and her political activism. Her passion for justice, including the fundamental right to education, led her to enroll in the doctoral program in human development and psychology at the Harvard University Graduate School of Education, from which she received a master's degree. She has been active in the Unitarian Universalist denomination for over twenty-five years and is a member of First Parish Watertown (Massachusetts). She continues her lifelong interests in quilting, embroidery, writing, growing flowers, and studying history. Reflecting on the courses she's taken in biology, chemistry, physics, epidemiology, and math, including two years of statistics, she now thinks of herself as a science nerd.

Demita Frazier, JD, is an unrepentant lifelong Black feminist, social justice activist, thought leader, writer, and teacher. A founding member of the Combahee River Collective, she has worked, in coalition with many, on the issues of reproductive rights, domestic violence, the care and protection of endangered children, urban sustainability issues affecting food access in poor and working-class communities, and a host of other important issues affecting communities of color. She has been a consistent advocate for the unequivocal freedom of Black women so that we can get on with the urgent business of freeing the world.

A 1986 graduate of Northeastern University School of Law, Frazier brought a Black feminist perspective to her work on environmental justice issues while working for the Office of Regional Counsel, the Environmental Protection Agency, as the Region 1 representative to the Federal Women's Commission.

Her current life goals include avid participation in the ongoing project of the dismantling of the myth of white supremacy, ending misogynoir and heteropatriarchal hegemony, and undermining late stage capitalism, with the hope of joining with others in creating a democratic socialist society. A practicing unallied Buddhist, she is committed to practicing loving kindness as she walks through life. A passionate cook and gardener, she would feed the world if she could.

 **Alicia Garza** is an organizer, writer, and freedom dreamer living and working in Oakland, CA. She is the special projects director for the National Domestic Workers Alliance, the nation's leading voice for dignity and fairness for the millions of domestic workers in the United States, most of whom are women. She is also the co-creator of #BlackLivesMatter, a national organizing project focused on combating anti-Black state-sanctioned violence. She has been the recipient of numerous awards, including the 2016 *Root* 100 list of African American achievers and influencers between the ages of twenty-five and forty-five, 2016 *Glamour* Women of the Year Award, and the 2016 *Marie Claire* New Guard Award, and was featured in

the *Politico* 50 guide to the thinkers, doers, and visionaries transforming American politics in 2015.

Barbara Ransby is an historian, writer, and longtime activist. She is a Distinguished Professor of African American studies, gender and women's studies, and history at the University of Illinois at Chicago (UIC), where she directs the campus-wide Social Justice Initiative. Ransby is author of the award-winning biography *Ella Baker and the Black Freedom Movement: A Radical Democratic Vision.* Her most recent book is *Eslanda: The Large and Unconventional Life of Mrs. Paul Robeson* (Yale University Press, January 2013). Ransby has also published in numerous scholarly and popular publications and lectures widely. In terms of her activism, Ransby was an initiator of the *African American Women in Defense of Ourselves* campaign in 1991, a co-convener of the Black Radical Congress in 1998, and a founder of Ella's Daughters, a network of women working in Ella Baker's tradition. In 2012 she became the second editor in chief of *SOULS*, a critical journal of Black politics, culture, and society published quarterly. In 2016, Barbara was elected president of the National Women's Studies Association (NWSA).

ABOUT HAYMARKET BOOKS

Haymarket Books is a radical, independent, nonprofit book publisher based in Chicago. Our mission is to publish books that contribute to struggles for social and economic justice. We strive to make our books a vibrant and organic part of social movements and the education and development of a critical, engaged, international left.

We take inspiration and courage from our namesakes, the Haymarket martyrs, who gave their lives fighting for a better world. Their 1886 struggle for the eight-hour day—which gave us May Day, the international workers' holiday—reminds workers around the world that ordinary people can organize and struggle for their own liberation. These struggles continue today across the globe—struggles against oppression, exploitation, poverty, and war.

Since our founding in 2001, Haymarket Books has published more than five hundred titles. Radically independent, we seek to drive a wedge into the risk-averse world of corporate book publishing. We are also the trade publishers of the acclaimed Historical Materialism Book Series and of Dispatch Books.

ALSO AVAILABLE FROM HAYMARKET BOOKS

A Beautiful Ghetto
Devin Allen, introductions
by Keeanga-Yamahtta Taylor
and D. Watkins

*Disposable Domestics: Immigrant
Women Workers in the Global Economy*
Grace Chang, foreword by Alicia
Garza, afterword by Ai-jen Poo

Feminist Freedom Warriors
Edited by Chandra Talpade
Mohanty and Linda Carty

*Women and Socialism:
Class, Race, and Capital*
Sharon Smith

*Freedom Is a Constant Struggle:
Ferguson, Palestine,
and the Foundations of a Movement*
Angela Y. Davis, edited by Frank
Barat, preface by Cornel West

*From #BlackLivesMatter
to Black Liberation*
Keeanga-Yamahtta Taylor

*Undivided Rights: Women of Color
Organize for Reproductive Justice*
Jael Silliman, Marlene Gerber
Fried, Loretta Ross,
and Elena Gutiérrez